Is There Life
after Analysis?

Is There Life after Analysis?

Dr. Alma H. Bond

Wynwood
A DIVISION OF
Baker Book House Co

©1993 by Alma H. Bond

Published by Wynwood Press,
a division of Baker Book House Company
P. O. Box 6287, Grand Rapids, Michigan 49516-6287

Printed in the United States of America

Library of Congress Cataloging-in-Publication Data

Bond, Alma Halbert.
    Is there life after analysis? / Alma H. Bond.
       p.   cm.
    ISBN 0-922066-88-4
    1. Psychotherapy—Termination. 2. Psychoanalysis. I. Title.
RC489.T45B665   1993
616.89' 14—dc20   93-14901

This book is dedicated
to **Lucy Freeman**

Contents

Preface

In my experience, at least four types of people are curious about psychoanalysis. The first group consists of those who are tempted to go into analysis but feel the need to know more about it before committing themselves. They are relatively fortunate, for many thousands of books, papers, and articles have been written on the subject by both professionals and laymen. Part 1 of this book, "The Fruits of Analysis," perhaps will add another note to the concerto.

The second group is made up of those people already in analysis who wish to know what they can expect in the future, having undergone such an intense experience. In particular, they want to know how analysis ends. How will I know when I am finished? is a question I have been asked many times. Another version of this query is asked by student analysts who have not yet finished their own analyses. How can I tell when my patient's analysis is over? they inquire.

A third group consists of individuals who have terminated analysis and wish to compare their results with those of others. Questions frequently asked by them include, Was I properly prepared for termination? What do I have the right to expect from my analysis? Is my experience typical? Am I lucky to have had the treatment I received, or have I the right to demand more? This is sometimes followed with, Should I go back into therapy, or are the results of my analysis all that can reasonably be expected? I have tried to answer the questions of groups two and three in part 2, "The Breaking-away Process."

Last of all, every analyst knows of people who have completed analysis but still are not content. Thoreau said, "Most people lead lives of quiet desperation." This may be as true for individuals who have completed analysis as for those who have never felt the need to enter therapy. Freud once said that the well-analyzed patient replaces neurotic illness with "plain, ordinary, everyday unhappiness." He meant that even though analysis may cure the symptoms of emotional illness, he could not guarantee that the analyzed patient would lead a happy life after the analysis is over. He felt that the exigencies of everyday life, such as the burdens of family responsibilities, making a living, illness, aging, and death leave people dissatisfied, disgruntled, and unfulfilled.

In my opinion this gloomy state of affairs can be as unnecessary as the neurosis it replaces. But to my knowledge, the only advice given by analysts to these discontented ex-patients is to return to analysis. I believe there is another way. Part 3 of this book, "Life after Analysis," is an attempt to answer the question of how to maintain a good state of mind after analysis is over. I hope you will find it useful.

Alma H. Bond

Acknowledgments

I would like to express appreciation to International Universities Press, the publishers of *Dream Portrait*, and to my co-authors, Dr. Arlene Kramer Richards and Dr. Daisy Franco for the use of material from *Dream Portrait* included in chapter 5. I am particularly indebted to Dr. Richards for permitting extensive use of her bibliography on the termination of analysis.

This book is unique in that it focuses on what takes place after the analysis is over, as well as on what leads to a successful termination. In particular, I wish to communicate my thanks and gratitude to those anonymous patients who have helped me understand the termination process and its aftermath over the many years of my psychoanalytic career. It is no truism to say that without them this book could never have been written.

Preserving the confidentiality of patients is a serious and difficult issue. On one hand it is absolutely essential; on the other, it is necessary to use what we have learned in our careers if it is to be passed on to future generations. I have done everything I could to protect the privacy of my patients without trivializing their analyses or their conflicts. Sometimes several patients have been combined into one. In all cases, identifying factors such as names, ages, appearances, backgrounds, nationality, marital status, number and sex of children, professions, position in the original family, and occasionally even the sex and race of the patient have been changed to the point where they are unrecognizable. What has been retained is only the inner truth as seen by me, and hopefully, by the patient.

I also want to express my indebtedness to the many writers whose ideas have contributed to this book, in particular Martin S. Bergmann, Marie Coleman Nelson, Dr. Arnold Z. Pfeffer, Michael E. Murray, Martha L. Murray, Patricia Garfield, Ann Faraday, Ella Freeman Sharpe, Margaret Mahler, and Faith Popcorn.

I want to thank my son, Jonathan Halbert Bond, president of Kirschenbaum and Bond Advertising Agency, for his generosity in allowing his agency to design the cover of the book.

Most of all I appreciate and am grateful to my friend and frequent co-author Lucy Freeman for her generous advice, encouragement, and support. She and I first plotted out this book together. In addition, she thought of the title before the manuscript was written. I fell in love with the title and was thus inspired to write the book.

Part 1

The Fruits of Analysis

1

How Analysis Changes Us

Analysis opens up the secret world of the self. This world lies buried deep inside because people feel ashamed or guilty about what they have done or wanted to do over the years. Analysis brings these submerged conflicts to consciousness and enables them to evaporate in the light of day.

The Rewards of Analysis

Successful analysis causes physiological changes in the brain that affect behavior, according to Dr. Theodore Reik, famous psychoanalyst. A vast quantity of energy is released that then can be used to meet inner needs. It takes a certain amount of courage for a patient to face the analyst at first, but the reward lies in gaining a new spirit and faith in the self.

Those who obtain analytic help lessen inner pain through deep understanding of its origin, which is primarily in their early years. Analysis enables them to realize that their wishes and cravings, often rooted in the past, are inappropriate in the lives of adults. When this is grasped on an emotional level, patients often are free to give up such cravings. The rewards of analysis, for both the patient and analyst, become increasingly heartening as life grows fuller, deeper, and enriched by the gratification of fulfilled dreams.

One woman patient said to me, gratitude in her voice, "I would be dead if I hadn't gone into analysis."

A man told me thankfully, "It's like I'm living a new life, one of which I am proud."

Many others have expressed gratitude for the role of analysis in improved emotional and physical health, professional success, and the development of new talents, skills, widened interests, and better relationships.

We might ask, What makes these analyses successful? What accounts for the changes in personality and character structure that lead to a positive outcome? What is it about the process that makes the changes it brings about deeper and more lasting than those found in other forms of therapy?

Why does analysis lead to a more fulfilled and less stressful life, one with less conflict, procrastination, and ambivalence? What enables many well-analyzed people to make a better choice of a mate? Why can people who have concluded an analysis often feel better, think better, and experience the harvest of their creativity? How is it that so many of our foremost professionals and artists have successfully completed such treatment?

Why is an analyzed person frequently in better physical health than before the analysis? What is it about successfully analyzed people that makes their lives different from the lives of others, to the point where it often is obvious to the eyes of the experienced observer?

This book will attempt to answer these questions. But first, let's look into the reasons people decide to be analyzed in the first place.

Reasons for Entering Analysis

Some say they enter analysis for intellectual reasons, perhaps to become analysts themselves. I do not believe this is a sufficient reason to motivate an analysand to endure the difficult stretches ahead. Such a person needs to understand that he or she has deep underlying difficulties as well as educational needs, in order to be successful in analysis.

Others come because their parents or mates have insisted. These cases usually do not work out unless the analyst can help them discover within themselves a deep-rooted need for change. I would not have accepted a patient for analysis who came for such a reason. If the disturbance is slight, the patient will be satisfied too easily with the relief experienced and will leave treatment before it is finished.

Such a patient will often waste the analyst's time and his own time and money with inconsequential trivia. He is not a good candidate for analysis and should seek a less demanding type of therapy. Freud spoke of such a case, in which a man inquired whether he should send his wife into analysis because she shaved off her pubic hair. Freud told the man to leave his wife alone. A person cannot be asked to open up his or her most intimate thoughts and feelings to a relative stranger unless the need is urgent. Rather, he or she must be in deep distress or emotional trouble to be willing to "play out the record."

Let us now look at some of the situations that bring people to analysis and carry a good prospect of being brought to a successful conclusion. Perhaps a primary relationship has failed and the individual does not understand why but only knows he or she cannot bear to continue a life of anguish and loneliness. One patient came for a serious analysis only when his fourth marriage fell apart. Before that, he always blamed his wives for the failure.

Another person may be self-defeating and cannot allow himself or herself to have anything in life that really matters. This character trait can lead to ruined relationships, education, and/or careers or may simply keep that person from experiencing the joys of everyday living.

Such a patient said to me, "I only get the things in life that are my second choice: my second-choice husband, second place in my graduating class, second prize at work, the second-greatest success." This woman, who was married to a renowned artist, wanted desperately to be famous herself. She became very successful financially but never made it to a hall of fame. In contrast, her husband had always wanted to be wealthy, but his paintings brought him only a modicum of money. Both partners were extremely successful, but not in the way they wanted most. Surely this was not a coincidence; rather, they could allow themselves to reap only the joys of second best.

An individual may be consumed with anxiety, either "free floating" or connected with a symptom like an obsession or compulsion. This may be serious enough to take over most of the person's life. One young man, a brilliant, handsome, personable playwright, was so obsessed with murderous thoughts he was unable to touch a pen to paper. Neither medication nor support groups helped this talented writer; only analysis was useful to him.

These days, another frequent reason for entering analysis is the feeling of a lack of identity. Some people wander aimlessly through life, without knowing who they are. This was poignantly expressed by Marjorie Mars, the patient to be discussed in chapter 4 as, "I feel like my face is without form, that if you stuck a pin in it, it might all run out."

Many come to analysis because they are depressed. They may not even use the word but complain that life seems gray, that whatever they experience brings them no pleasure. Conversation is boring to them, sex a chore, work something to be endured until five o'clock, plays and movies leave them cold. One chronically depressed woman illustrated this well when she said that to her, all food seemed tasteless. Sometimes, when the depression is bad enough, even medication may not work. Or the periods of depression seem to recur without any rhyme or reason. Then analysis may seem the only alternative to suicide.

Other people, including those referred by physicians, come to analysis because of psychosomatic illness. Some wear their tensions in their muscles, while others conceal their psychic pain in their bloodstream or their intestines. Whatever the location of the physical problem, it is remarkable to observe that many patients become relatively disease-proof during the course of analysis. I have seen improvements in my patients in the symptoms, among other illnesses, of allergies, colitis, constipation, diarrhea, obesity, respiratory illness, sinus infections, back pain, and in particular the frequency of colds and flu, as their analyses proceeded.

As Lucy Freeman stated in her book *Fight Against Fears,* she first went into analysis when her physician recommended that she seek psychoanalytic treatment because her nose had been so clogged for a year that she could hardly breathe. During her first session, she burst into tears that became a torrent.

According to Lucy, "After the hour ended, I stood up to leave. Suddenly I discovered I felt strangely light-headed. My hands flew to my nose. I shouted, 'I can breathe!'

"I took a deep breath through nostrils that had been clogged for a year. It felt as though a thick gag had been ripped from my mouth, heavy chains torn from my ankles.

"'You have wanted to cry but couldn't,' the analyst said. 'The tear ducts got dammed up and affected your nasal passages.'

"'That's a direct relationship between the physical and the emotional, isn't it?' I asked, suddenly understanding the feel of the word *psychosomatic*."

Many people believe there is even a psychosomatic component in the development of cancer. It is interesting that in the course of my forty-year career as a psychoanalyst, not one patient became ill with cancer during his or her analysis proper.

A recent article in the *Miami Herald* bears out the hypothesis of a psychosomatic component of cancer—in this case skin cancer. According to the article, "Skin cancer patients in a short-term psychological program showed better coping and mood five years later [than other cancer patients], as well as an unexplained reduction in cancer recurrence."[1]

Other psychological ailments known to have yielded to analysis are anxiety neuroses, panic states, phobias, tics, uneven psychosexual development, difficulties in speech and language such as stuttering, substance abuse, separation anxiety, schizophrenia, sadomasochism, sexual dysfunctions such as inhibitions of arousal and orgasm, exhibitionism and voyeurism, sleep problems, deficiencies in impulse control such as kleptomania, and multiple personality, post-traumatic stress, and borderline and narcissistic disorders. In addition, I have found analysis, along with psychotropic medication, to be helpful to patients suffering from schizophrenia and manic depression or bipolar disorders.

All of these people are proper candidates for analysis, when they also are courageous, intelligent, introspective, lucky, and find themselves the right analyst.

I went into analysis forty years ago because I became emotionally ill. It became increasingly difficult to go out by myself, yet I found it intolerable to ride in a bus unless I could sit alone. Mostly I stayed home and read analytic books in the attempt to cure myself. One of the books was Karen Horney's *Self Analysis.*[2] Someone once said that book brought more people into analysis than any other in history. Add me to the list.

I know now that my situation was even worse than I realized at the time. I have recorded some of my dreams since I was twenty-one, the year my younger brother died of cerebral meningitis. In a dream of that period—one of the first I collected—a crazy woman was about to attack me with a knife. I didn't realize it at the time, but now I know the "crazy woman" was me. I feel very lucky that I didn't become psychotic or suicidal.

One day I had to admit I couldn't do it alone. Anyway, I rationalized, it wasn't because of my weakness I was seeking help; analysis was a prerequisite for further training. I made an appointment with Dr. J., a man recommended by the institute where I was studying. That analysis was not a success. I know now that Dr. J. overintellectualized and had no real empathy for me.

But a second analysis five years later indeed cured my illness. This analyst was much more effective. Dr. Z. was a motherly, charismatic Viennese refugee who had begun her career at the age of fifty after arriving in the United States. She was a highly intuitive woman who understood me very well. I felt better immediately, and my symptoms disappeared within a matter of weeks. The analysis successfully ended five years later. I was by then a happily married mother of three, studying for my doctorate at Columbia University, securely ensconced in a rewarding career of the practice of psychoanalysis. The analysis had done everything for me I had asked for. But now that I am older, I can see that there are many bonuses to a successful analysis that are almost as rewarding as the original cure. The fruits of analysis are ripening in me still.

The Fruits of Analysis

Most of all it seems to me that when analysis works well, life gets simpler. If one is less conflicted, there is much less agonizing over taking action. The analyzed person is more able to say, "This is what I want. There is no reason why I shouldn't try to get it. So that is what I am going to do." In Lucy Freeman's case, relieved of the necessity to waste time with neurotic stalling, she found herself able to write three books a year instead of one.

Before my analysis (I don't count the first one) I was full of conflict. For starters, there was the full year I spent reading psychoanalytic books in hopes of finding a "cure." The rest of the time I yearned for what I couldn't have, either because the time for it was long past or it had never existed at all. I was obsessed with jealousy over what seemed like life's unfairness.

When I was born, I was the queen of the household. My mother used to say that people brought gifts much as when Jesus was born. But little did I know that my reign was only temporary. For when I was three years old, a little brother was born who immediately became my mother's favorite. Suddenly I was dethroned; it was only the baby who mattered. Like Cinderella, I felt relegated to the attic. I seemed to get over the difficulty well enough, however, to go about my childhood successfully. But when my brother died, the entire conflict was revived. Much of it was unconscious; I only knew that I felt cheated and unhappy much of the time. When analysis assuaged the need for outgrown gratifications and mitigated the anger wrought by their absence, I felt enriched by time. There was a whole new life to go about as I wished, now that I was relatively free of conflict.

As part of the emancipation from neurosis, analyzed people seem to be more distanced from their parents. Instead of remaining embroiled in old jealousies, competitions, infantile love, and/or abiding hatred of them, people who have successfully completed analysis are able to outgrow infantile ties with their families and go on to more mature relationships. In the case of John Jones, the "hero" of *Dream Portrait,* [3] who is discussed in chapter 5, his entire inner feelings about his parents changed. Instead of a vicious, punitive father out to get him, John now saw an old man who within the limits of his personality had done the best he could for his son. And rather than an enslaving seductress, he now viewed his mother as a very nice lady who had been adored by her little Oedipus.

My parents died years ago. I think of them now and then, usually with fondness. Sometimes I am sad that they are not around to share the joys of watching their grandchildren grow up, or to read the books that I have written. But in an important sense I have left them behind with my analysis; they are not an omnipresent part of my life.

When people experience less conflict, they have more energy available for the important business of living. Instead of endlessly reiterating past woes in the years following my analysis I was able to raise three children, finish my doctorate, and become a full-fledged psychoanalyst. A friend said I seemed to do all this "with my little finger." But I think it is just that in analysis one learns to distinguish the important from the nonessential.

For example, during those years a group of acquaintances was into giving little gourmet dinner parties, vying with one another as to who could cook and serve the finest meals. For some individuals such parties are an art, a delight that adds richness to their lives. But for me winning this contest was not worth the time and effort, so I stopped seeing those people as a group and had lunch at a restaurant with the ones I cared about. Looking back now I know this was the right choice for me. My measure has always been, Do these actions add up? Or will I bemoan on my deathbed the waste of a lifetime? Will I say, along with Wordsworth, "We have given our hearts away, a sordid boon"?[4] For me, all the thousands of efforts involved in raising a child or building a fine career add up gloriously, while giving little gourmet dinner parties does not.

Perhaps the reverse is true for you. If so, you would do well to develop your talents for gourmet cooking at the expense of what you feel is less important. Analysis has freed me to spend my time writing. In contrast, a friend of mine has stopped writing letters. She doesn't enjoy corresponding, only reluctantly having done so out of duty all her life. "You have learned to write, and I am learning not to," she said, perhaps by way of apology. Although the loss is truly mine, I was able to answer, "Very good. We each have to do what we have to do."

Another example of what has fallen by the wayside for me is sculpting. I have a small talent for it and enjoy doing it. But it is not the way I want to spend my life. I also would like to learn to play the violin, to take a course in quantum physics, and to earn a Ph.D. in English literature. But the time left is growing shorter by the moment. Perhaps if I had another lifetime. . . . But I do know that for me to give elegant little dinner parties or to jam sculpting into an already overpacked day is simply too expensive emotionally.

A further example of how we can get in our own way is evident in the case of my former patient Mrs. K. Although she had been married for years and was very attached to her husband, analysis made it clear that she had to fight her husband's negativism for everything she wanted, from taking a taxi home to going on the vacation of her choice. She was appalled to discover that literally half their time together was wasted arguing about whether she was wrong in wanting what she wanted. When analysis revealed that unconscious guilt made it difficult for her to feel that she deserved to get what she wanted, Mrs. K. no longer needed her husband to control her spending habits. She was able to leave him and establish a new, more reasonable life in which she was free to decide what was important to her. This, incidentally, did not include wasting half her life in futile, unnecessary arguments.

Dr. Gladys Natchez, one of my closest friends, was so changed by analysis that she appears to be a different person. In her young-adult years, she was stiff and unnatural. Her rigid bouffant hairdo was indicative of her personality. She had very little self-confidence and was meek and unsure of herself. When she spoke, it was generally in an effort to please the person with whom she was talking. Then came a true metamorphosis. As she poetically put it, "I'm searching and changing all the time, while, like the river, I'm still the same."

Gladys is now a bold, self-confident woman, who is known for her outspokenness. She believes in honesty at all costs. Whenever possible, what she feels is what she says, for she has the courage of her convictions. For example, one of her friends, May, took up painting, and asked if Gladys thought she showed any talent. She responded by simply saying, "No." While one would not like to be May under these circumstances, perhaps in the long run Gladys was doing her friend a service. In any case, one must admire her for standing behind her principles.

Gladys stresses that there are aspects of herself she does not wish to change. She says she is aware of her limitations as well as her assets but feels she would be lost without both. She says, "I am all of me—take it or leave it." Perhaps this ability itself is another aspect of change, for she now accepts all facets of her nature, not only the traits that are "good."

Perhaps even a deeper change came about in Mary, one of my earliest patients. She was a young woman who entered analysis with suicidal urges and deep regressive tendencies.

She would hang around my doorstep long after the end of her analytic hour. My husband used to meet her outside the door and feel sorry for her. At the height of her treatment, she would soak in a warm bathtub for twenty-four hours a day, getting up only to come for treatment. There she would have fantasies that she was a suckling infant nursing at my breast. The analysis helped Mary to experience her fantasies to the fullest and enjoy them as if they were real. Then she was able to renounce them, for analysis had given her some of the gratification she craved in a manner that was acceptable to the adult woman.

Mary's mother had been a cold, unyielding woman who lived according to strict and rigid rules. Mary does not remember her mother ever holding her in her arms or speaking tenderly to her. A typical example of the way she was raised is revealed in the following anecdote: Eight-year-old Mary was helping her mother peel some tomatoes. The intelligent child thought of a way to peel the tomatoes that would save more of their meat. With excitement she told her mother what she had figured out. Her mother was quiet for a moment, and then in her stony manner answered the child, "Keep peeling!" It is easy to understand why Mary was submerged by her yearning for a warm and generous mother.

After a long and painful analysis, Mary finally was able to come to terms with the fact that her analyst could never be her mother. She fought the knowledge for years, until she grew to understand that even if the analyst were able to fill that role, Mary really did not want to be a baby again. She was able to leave her analysis successfully and marry and have children of her own, to whom she gave the love and affection she herself had never experienced. Mary has become a healthy human being who leads a full life and is a highly successful attorney.

As previously suggested, life seems easier for the well-analyzed person, in line with the biblical pronouncement, "To him who hath shall be given." This was borne out recently in a short space of time when I coauthored two articles, each with a different individual. The first writer was rigid, perfectionistic, argumentative, and obstructionistic. In contrast, the second was hardworking yet pliant, willing to concede points yet far from wishy-washy about what she believed to be correct. The first author was a nightmare to work with, critical, demanding, and verbose, insisting on her own point of view even when it was obvious she was wrong. I never will work with her again. The second coauthor was a delight and pleasant to work with. We wasted no time in power struggles or neurotic complications but immediately got down to business and finished the article in no time flat. The second author was analyzed by one of the great psychoanalysts of all time. If the first person was analyzed at all, she should return for a repeat performance.

As a result of the emotional distancing from one's parents, a most important change frequently comes about in the kind of person one "chooses" to love. The love that develops for a person during or after treatment is based on different conditions than those responsible for the choosing of lovers before therapy.

In a successful analysis, the patient's original love objects have been at least partially replaced by the figure of the analyst. Then the patient reenacts the illness, which originated in childhood, with the analyst in the leading role. When the repetition is made conscious by the more objective figure of the analyst, the patient is able to see what "really happened" and becomes accessible to change. As the relationship with the analyst is resolved, the individual becomes free of his neurotic ties to figures of the past. Since one's original loves have then become less emotionally impelling, the type of person selected for a new love object often changes.

In analysis, each new phase of love for the analyst is based on the activation of an infantile prototype. As the process uncovers hitherto repressed material, hopefully the old needs for the person who was all-important in childhood are outgrown, and the patient both during and after analysis is free to develop a new kind of love. As one grows to understand what motivated the old attachment, the new love often will be based on different, more mature conditions than existed before treatment.

A good example is the case of Agnes, who had been married to an alcoholic, asexual, self-involved New Yorker. After analysis helped her understand that the motivation for her choice was his emotional resemblance to her painfully unavailable father, she consciously set out to select a man who was the absolute opposite of her first husband. The second man was a large, blond, cheery midwesterner who loved the out-of-doors. He was and is absolutely devoted to Agnes. It appeared to both analyst and patient that her new love was based on positive memories of her father and uncles, as well as more recent experiences with the analyst. Because the new relationship was all that she discovered she needed, they decided not to have any children. Today Agnes is the center of her husband's life. The arrangement apparently is what he needs too, for they are one of the happiest couples I know.

Another frequent result of analysis is that the physical health of the successfully analyzed patient greatly improves. Colds and flu, as do more severe illnesses, crop up much less frequently. The well-analyzed person is more aware of his or her emotional conflicts and has less need to repress them. Therefore, there is less pressure for buried needs to burst through the bounds of the unconscious in symptoms of illness. This was beautifully expressed in a quote collected by the renowned Cuban scholar Lydia Cabrera, during her conversations with Afro-Cubans: "If the heart is healthy, the body seldom will be sick."[5]

Many of my patients have completed an entire analysis without ever having missed a single session for illness. This was also my own experience both in and after analysis. One patient said about me, "In five years, never a cold, not even a cough. How in the world does she do it?"

A good example of the recovery of physical health through the unearthing of buried feelings can be seen in the case of Henrietta, an unmarried thirty-year-old woman who had suffered all her adult life from colitis. The disease relentlessly constricted her existence and caused her much suffering and humiliation. She rarely was able to leave home, as "accidents" were as likely to occur as not. The illness interfered with her sexual gratification as much as her social life, as she felt disgusting and unattractive to men.

During her analysis Henrietta became aware that her mother had been literally crazy on the subject of the bowels. She took cathartics herself every day and frequently gave her daughter enemas even when she was well. An illustration of the degree of the woman's obsession is that she administered Ex-Lax even to the family dog. But most important to Henrietta was the fact that she and her mother had virtually no other physical contact from the time she was an infant. Nor did her mother seem very interested in her in other ways. Henrietta was unaware that contact of any type with her mother was preferable to none at all; she knew only that she dreaded and fought the enemas with all her might. In her deepest unconscious, however, she derived gratification from the enemas as the only way she and her mother could feel close. The ordeal provided both physical intimacy and sexual excitement for both participants. It also induced in Henrietta the horror and helplessness of a rape, as many times her father held the struggling child down while her mother administered the enema.

In her analysis it became apparent that the colitis attacks reproduced the enemas for Henrietta, in that she had to hold the watery feces in her body until she no longer could bear it. Then she was humiliated by her lack of control, just as she had been in childhood when the fecal matter burst out of her body. In addition, the physician's treatment of choice was for her to administer steroid enemas to herself! When she understood the hidden determinants of her illness, the colitis attacks gradually lessened and then all but disappeared.

Lingerie was very important to Henrietta, for all of her adult life she had to wear pads to keep from soiling her undergarments. She was not inclined to wear beautiful lingerie only to have it stained during her accidents. As she got better, she didn't have to go to the bathroom so often, had no more accidents, and was relieved of the necessity of wearing pads. Then she was able to gloat, "Now I can wear beautiful underwear like everyone else." As a graduation-from-analysis present, she bought for herself the most beautiful and expensive lingerie she could find.

Henrietta also had come into treatment for a severe depression, which also had originated in the deprivation of her childhood. By the termination of her analysis, Henrietta's depression was greatly alleviated. She had learned how to take better care of her health and to dress beautifully. She had found the ability to experience more joy in her accomplishments and her life in general. She now could go out with men. She also developed her interest in music and began a new career. Most important of all, Henrietta completed the termination of her analysis without experiencing a recurrence of her colitis.

Carrie had a different set of health problems. She was an extremely obese young woman of twenty-three who had been sent to many therapists and psychiatrists but had proved unwilling to stay with any of them. To the surprise of her parents, she immediately developed a strong rapport with me and was entering into her third year of therapy at the time of this account.

Her treatment revealed that her mother was a very infantile, dependent woman with a whiplash for a tongue and, not so incidentally, a lovely figure, who had leaned on her daughter all her life. As a result, Carrie felt that she never had a childhood. From the time she was very small, she had to serve as her mother's mother if she wanted any maternal relationship other than a battered one. This left her starved for mothering, so to speak, and she ate her way to severe illness. Food was the one source of nurturing that could always be depended on, and her constant need for nurturing kept her eating constantly.

The propensity to obesity was also caused by the fact that she was terrified of men and sex. She became aware, among other things, that being grossly overweight served to ward off men. When she met men who were not discouraged by her appearance, she still felt that her looks were repulsive and this turned off her own sexual drive. As a result she had never had a lover, or even a boyfriend. Therapeutically, all went well, as Carrie learned more and more about herself and the reasons for her obesity.

In terms of health, though, all was not well. Carrie weighed over three hundred pounds, and her blood pressure was sky-high. Bright and talented as she was, nobody would give her a job because she was such a poor health risk. She had been told by her physician that her life would be considerably shortened by the effects of obesity on her heart, lungs, and vital organs. By this time she could not even walk down the street without having to stop to breathe. In my office I had to remove all the pillows of a large armchair before she could fit into it. She was terribly humiliated by her weight when she had to purchase two airplane seats for herself and couldn't go to the movies because the seats were too small to accommodate her.

My feeling was that her weight problem would be the last of her symptoms to go. I believed that as she gained insight into her need for mothering and fear of sex, the pounds would dwindle away. Yet analysis takes a long time, particularly in so disturbed an individual as Carrie. Her life was on hold until she lost weight. Because she could not get a job, she was forced to be financially dependent on her family. And she could not form the loving relationship she craved. I felt very sorry for her as one person after another rejected her bids for both a job and friendship.

Even worse, I felt her very life was at stake. Therefore, when her physician suggested an intestinal by-pass procedure whereby a portion of her intestines would be removed, both Carrie and I, as well as her parents, agreed that surgery was the treatment of choice. As a result of such surgery, much less food is absorbed by the intestines, and a quick weight loss can be expected. Carrie was quite excited about the idea. She had worked through her expectations of and anxieties about surgery, as well as her fear of sexuality, so that she felt ready to form a relationship with a man. She was determined to see the operation through. It seemed to me a good and healthy decision for so young a woman whose life was in danger from her illness.

Carrie then visited Dr. Helman Paris, a surgeon who specialized in intestinal by-pass cases, and told him her story.

I was shocked a few days after their consultation to receive the following letter and report:

Dear Dr. Bond:

I am writing you on behalf of your patient, Carrie Carter, whom we have seen in consultation concerning the advisability of intestinal by-pass surgery. We have administered an intensive battery of tests, which indicate she is physically well-suited for an intestinal by-pass procedure. I am concerned, however, with her emotional state and her possible reactions to the intense gastrointestinal discomfort, such as nausea, weakness, diarrhea, rectal pain, and soreness, and in particular the changes in body image that follow such a process. After many years of this type of surgery I have come to the conclusion that the by-pass procedure often presents a grave psychological danger to a person like Carrie. We have had some rather unpleasant incidents that occurred when patients discovered their surgery did not give them the kind of body image they expected. In certain cases we have even found it necessary to reconnect the intestine in patients who became seriously depressed or who refused to cooperate with the close medical supervision we consider imperative for the avoidance of metabolic problems.

Therefore, with Carrie's permission and indeed at her request, we have sent her for a consultation with Dr. Morris Herbert, a highly qualified young psychiatrist. Enclosed you will find a copy of the results of the consultation. I understand Miss Carter has been in treatment with you for some time. I would not like to undertake such surgery on her without your opinion as to whether she is emotionally mature enough to withstand the trauma of an intestinal by-pass operation. We would particularly like your assessment as to whether she is stable enough to adequately cope with the changes that occur after surgery. Would you be kind enough to give me your reaction to Dr. Herbert's report as soon as possible, as the patient is quite eager to undertake the surgery?

After receiving your response we will continue our evaluation and advise her as to our decision. Thank you for your cooperation.

Sincerely yours,
Helman K. Paris, M.D.

Dr. Herbert's report, in part, was as follows:

Miss Carrie Carter, a vivacious, amiable, cooperative, neatly dressed, and exceptionally obese twenty-three-year-old Caucasian female, consulted with me as to the desirability of her undertaking intestinal by-pass surgery. Her orientation to time, place, person, and situation is satisfactory. I found her to be quite slick and articulate. Her affect was usually composed although she dissolved into anxious crying when she stated that she felt a delay in her surgery could have disastrous effects. When asked to explain what she meant, she intellectualized that surgery causes anxiety because she has never had any, that her heart muscle is being stretched by her obesity, and that rapid surgery might prolong her life. I feel Miss Carter has some magical expectations of the surgery, expecting it to solve all her life problems.

She speaks in a highly controlled manner, and stresses that she is ready for the surgery and deeply desirous of having it as soon as possible. Her presentation is given in highly guarded tones, as she attempts to force this information on the interviewer.

Miss Carter seeks to give the impression that she is an autonomous young woman who understands the psychic problems that have caused her obesity and present lack of friends. She presents herself as a mature person who has gained independence from her parents. However, she lives in the same building as her parents, and I suspect she is more dependent on them than she indicates. It also seems to me she is more dependent on her analyst than a well-analyzed individual who has largely worked through her problems in separation would be. Also, I am gravely concerned about her urgency to have the surgery performed immediately.

In conclusion, I suspect that Miss Carter is a far more pathologically dependent personality than she would have me believe and that she has magical expectations for the surgery. In my professional opinion these infantile characteristics would seriously impede her recovery and the opportunity for a successful outcome of the surgery. I personally hesitate to recommend any unnecessary surgery for so immature an individual.

Yours truly,
Morris Herbert, M.D.

I had a strange reaction to these letters: I was furious! Despite the necessity for caution in medical procedures, I felt the psychiatric report was written by a verbose, inexperienced psychiatrist who was showing off to "Big Daddy" in the hope of getting more referrals. I was particularly offended by his use of jargon, such as his description of this vital, courageous, imaginative, thoughtful, far-seeing young woman as "female," "slick," "Caucasian," displaying "affect," "controlled," who "intellectualized" her feelings and had "magical expectations." Wouldn't he be anxious if he were twenty-three years old and undergoing his first serious operation?

In my opinion, Carrie was more realistic than these doctors. She had been told by her family physician that her life was in danger, and her zest for living propelled her toward surgery as the only way she knew to help herself at that time. She lived in the same building as her parents because rent-controlled apartments were extremely scarce in New York City, and the landlord was kind enough to give one to the daughter of tenants who had occupied their apartment for over twenty years. As far as dependency on her analyst is concerned, Carrie never presented herself as being finished with analysis. The dependency is necessary to work out relationship problems in the treatment. The psychiatrist should have known about this transference. By the time her analysis is completed, we will have resolved the dependency.

I wrote to Dr. Paris telling him my feelings. He accepted my professional opinion and scheduled the surgery shortly thereafter. Carrie experienced no untoward difficulties after the operation and convalesced easily and quickly. As a matter of fact, she finally got some nurturing she needed when her mother came to the hospital and took care of her. She lost 115 pounds the year after the surgery and has continued to lose weight ever since.

William's change through analysis was of a completely different order. He was highly intelligent, in fact a scholar of Shakespeare. An attractive man of thirty-eight, he had come into analysis in a deeply depressed state. According to him, he always built up the women he was interested in. Then when they became people in their own right, they always left him. He complained that he couldn't feel and had no sensation at all in his penis during intercourse. Since he was convinced no one he loved could ever love him, he believed he had nothing to live for. The only way he could go on living, he said, was to keep a loaded gun in the antique English cabinet by his bed. Then he knew that if things got worse, he could kill himself and/or any man who attacked him.

William's mother was a sweet, loving, perhaps naive woman who he felt preferred him to her other four children. But his father was a highly critical, sadistic man who had disparaged William all his life, perhaps because of jealousy of his brilliant son. As a result, William couldn't allow himself to enjoy his mother's love and attention, for he always was on guard for the anticipated assault by his father. William transferred this fear to all male authorities and was usually miserable with his teachers and his boss.

One day he brought the gun into his session in his briefcase. I was very frightened and told him to take it out to the foyer, as I found it impossible to work under that kind of anxiety. To my relief, he listened and took the briefcase out of the room. Shortly after, he brought me the bullets and asked if he could leave them with me. I agreed. It was at this point that I knew he was going to get well. William had learned that not all authorities are out to demolish him, and he no longer felt the need to protect himself with a loaded gun. At the present time he is close friends with his boss, with whom William behaves as an equal. He has faced his fear of homosexuality, as well as of going insane, and realizes he is unlikely to actively experience either state. In addition, his relationship with all the members of his family, including his father, has improved. He no longer monopolizes his mother, and his father and siblings hate him less for it. He enjoys sex with his wife and is the delighted father of a beautiful baby boy.

Scholars ordinarily have less income than they deserve. William left analysis owing me money, the installments of which he paid regularly. I did not hear from him until a few years after he left treatment, when I received the following letter, enclosing his final payment:

Dear Dr. Bond:

Excuse the delay in writing you, but I wanted to pay off my debt to you first.

You were right—I do not feel a sense of having been "ripped away" from you like Macduff, who "from his mother's womb was untimely ripp'd." Your teachings are alive in me. I cannot always listen to them, but they help make deep despair a stranger to me.

Confidence in my decisions grows as I get more and more pleasure out of my work. When I came into analysis, I was a man like King Lear, who "hath ever but slenderly known himself." Under your guidance I have learned to look into my deepest self. Unlike Lear, I often like what I see.

I am not so sure Marilyn Monroe would have ended as she did if she had had you for an analyst.

With heartfelt love and appreciation for you for your faith in me, for my rebirth, and for your patience.

William

I often can tell if someone I meet has been analyzed. The first time this happened was when I met a woman who I later learned was a fine analyst. The conversation we had was a simple one that touched not at all on analytic topics. Yet without being told, it seemed to me that her "insides" were steadier, that she lived in a smooth emotional 'space with fewer hooks and gaps than most of us inhabit. I couldn't tell what conflicts she had overcome, but I knew somehow that she had. This experience was to be repeated many times since. I suppose I might have missed one now and then, but the conviction that I am in the presence of a successfully analyzed person never has been proven wrong.

Before my analysis, I was a conscience-ridden individual who was always doing what I was supposed to do. If a decision was to be made as to how to spend my time, I usually decided on what I believed was good for me. Or on what my family would like me to do. Or on what I thought I should do to make others feel more comfortable. This kind of personality might be great for others to have around, but it is not conducive to individual happiness. Believe me, I know from personal experience. One summer I had a neighbor who was like that. Her husband loved boats. She hated them. But she thought a good wife always did what her husband wanted. He liked her to go fishing with him. So every day she went out on his boat. And every night she came home and got drunk. While my case was not as extreme as my neighbor's, I must say I tended in that direction. As a result, I was not the fulfilled person I have become since.

My present life as a writer is an example of my postanalytic philosophy. I was a psychoanalyst for forty years. I have always loved the process of analysis. No matter what my mood each morning, I could cross my office threshold knowing that at least one incident would give me pleasure the rest of the day. But in recent years, I gradually realized that I no longer could spend my time doing this work I loved. Life is short and death is long, and my writing needs were unfulfilled. So I terminated my practice and moved to Key West, where I spend my days at the computer. Here I write the books that have "blushed unseen" all of my adult life. Now my fulfillment comes from the writing, and not from my work with patients. I am not dependent on them for gratification, but only on my own creativity. As a result, I never have been more content.

Freud, in *Civilization and Its Discontents*, asks what people want from life, what do they show by their behavior to be the purpose and intention of their lives. He answers, "They strive after happiness; they want to be happy and to remain so." But in this purpose, he continues, we are at loggerheads with the whole world, for if each of us were to do what we want all the time, the result would be chaos, if not total destruction.[6]

Indeed, civilized man has exchanged a portion of his potentiality for happiness for a safety net of security. Otherwise the very fabric of our lives would be dominated by the strongest and most ruthless individuals. The downside to this security is that a person who cannot tolerate the amount of frustration imposed by society becomes unhappy, if not neurotic. "Everything I want to do is either immoral, illegal, or fattening" is a modern restatement of the same philosophy.

A good part of the human struggle centers on the task of finding some sort of accommodation between individual wants and the claims of the group. Such a compromise is best found in following one's own wishes whenever possible.

In consequence of my own postanalytic experiences, I have tried for many years to help patients understand that the path to happiness lies along that of gratifying their own wishes whenever they can. I suggest you live that way too.

Perhaps at the present time you are not able to make major changes in your life. We cannot always do what we want when we want to do it, no matter how important the need. But there are countless small decisions during the day when we can follow the path of our impulses. Do you want to make your bed now, or would you rather wait till after breakfast? Make your bed later. It doesn't matter one whit when the bed gets made, but your own contentment is priceless. Do you really want to go to that party, or are you afraid the hostess will be angry with you if you stay home and read the book you've been hoarding for weeks? Do you feel like writing letters now, or would you rather take a walk in the park? Take your walk. There may come a moment later when writing letters is exactly what you want to do. And at that time you will enjoy writing them much more. Incidentally, the results probably will show it.

President Bush expressed a similar sentiment in a negative fashion when he said, "I'm president of the United States, and if I don't like broccoli, I don't have to eat it!" A friend of mine once verbalized an analogous feeling when she returned some food she didn't like in a restaurant. "I make one hundred thousand dollars a year," she said, "and if I don't like something, I'm not going to eat it."

I once asked a famous analyst, "How much does a person need to make up for early deprivation?" The analyst answered, "As much as he can get!" I agree, but would reword the answer, "As much as he can give to himself."

The Goal of Analysis

In attempting to answer the question, What makes analysis successful? Shakespeare's lines come to mind, "To thine own self be true. And . . . [then] thou canst not then be false to any man." Above all, an analyzed person has learned to be true to himself or herself. In a way, this is the goal of analysis, to teach the patient to face what he or she really feels or thinks without the subterfuges, deceits, and manipulations that fill the lives of less privileged people.

Most of us have been brought up to believe that sexual and angry feelings are "bad" and should not even be felt. In addition it is very difficult to allow oneself to experience feelings of terror, grief, loneliness, guilt, shame, and pain, particularly when one must face them alone. So, over the years, we have devised ways to push these feelings out of awareness. Among other means, we repress them, deny them, distort them, impart them to others, and turn them into painful physical symptoms. We limit our lives and our pleasures for the proverbial mess of pottage. Although these efforts may result in temporary relief, in the long run it is poor emotional economy. For it often results in emotional dishonesty, neurosis, physical illness, and/or difficulties in getting along with others.

Try as we will, we cannot be honest with ourselves or others when the true reasons for our behavior are buried in the unconscious. Unearthing them is essential for the achievement of true emotional honesty. When we do not lie to ourselves, life becomes easier, less complicated, less conflicted. To this analyst and former analysand, the rewards of undergoing the often arduous and expensive process of analysis are well worth the effort. The compensations are gargantuan indeed. I cannot imagine living in any other way.

Part **2**

The Breaking-away Process

Preparing for
the Termination of Analysis

"The purpose of analysis is to finish," is the way one very astute patient put it. He was quite right; in one way the entire analysis is a preparation for its eventual termination. Every exploration and interpretation by the analyst, in the long run, is to enable the patient to survive better on his or her own after the analysis is over. Insofar as it resolves dependency on the analyst, raises self-esteem, tames grandiosity, "softens" or "hardens" the conscience, outmodes the infantile, and examines monsters of the past in the light of the present day, each intervention helps ready the patient to leave.

What, specifically, can the analyst do to prepare a patient for termination? Above all, he or she can analyze the patient well. Some people are afraid that analysis will lead to greater dependence and thus will never end. Not true. Such patients have come into therapy because of unresolved dependency needs; they were not instilled in them by analysis. No one wishes to be dependent forever. Hence any successful analysis eventually will lead to its own conclusion. Again, the purpose of analysis is to finish. It is interesting that the forty-five-year-old man who made this remark was enabled by his analysis to learn to love. As a result, he formed a stable relationship with a woman for the first time in his life, and left the analysis after his marriage. His purpose in analysis was indeed to finish, and he was able to do so successfully in a relatively short time.

Just as a good parent allows his children ever greater independence, so a good analyst will assist his or her patients along the road to autonomy long before termination begins. At the start of an analysis, I help patients a great deal in their associations, particularly with their dreams. But as they get more independent, they take over the dream work almost entirely. John Jones (see chapter 5) said late in his analysis, "In the beginning you helped me with my dreams; now you let me do them myself." In this and similar ways the analyst weans the patient for life after analysis.

In my opinion, the best description of how the analyst goes about preparing the patient for termination is given by Marie Coleman Nelson,[1] who states that she infers from the outset of treatment that the patient, conscious of it or not, both wants to leave and wants to stay. She finds the latter is an inevitable factor in every resistance against a successful analysis.

Marie Coleman Nelson does not believe that the termination process begins in the last phase, but treats the entire therapeutic process as "an ongoing series of hellos and good-byes." Even when the question of separating is far from the thoughts of the patient, she manages to get across that "life, traffic accidents, icy roads, and nuclear hazards being what they are, each session spent together may be our last—just as I communicate that within my powers I am available for as long as we can tolerate each other and the patient benefits from therapy." She feels that separation whether by natural or unnatural causes is an intrinsic part of life and must be dealt with throughout therapy to immunize the patient against eventual termination as well as other separations he or she inevitably will experience.

Marie Coleman Nelson believes that it is possible to convey the message subtly, even when it is not central in the patient's thinking. She does this partly by use of such proverbs as "Here today, gone tomorrow!" Such responses, she states, tend "to evoke the grim images that we all seek to suppress."

How do patients react to the idea of termination of analysis? In as many ways as there are people. One thing is certain: People respond to the ending of treatment in the same manner in which they have faced previous traumata. Those who have denied their anxiety and dread under other circumstances will refuse to admit that they care about leaving. For example, a person who disclaims illness and goes to work with a raging fever may protest that he is happy to leave the analysis, that he will have more time, more money, and so on, and does not expect to miss the analyst. When the leavetaking is too comfortable, the experienced analyst will get suspicious and seek to help the patient find and experience the hidden grief beneath his defenses. If he leaves without going through a mourning period, he is in line for trouble later. Such unresolved issues might cause a person to become disillusioned about psychoanalysis, to fall into a deep depression, or develop another painful symptom. In all likelihood, he will need to return to analysis for further treatment. Similarly, people who escape pain through an addiction will feel the urge to return to the drug, food, or alcohol that brought them into treatment. Likewise, those who have suffered from obsessions or compulsions may well experience a return of their symptoms.

Some patients who are perfectionists are dissatisfied with the results of their analysis. Analyzed or not, we still are human beings, with all our shortcomings and frailties, although hopefully with fewer than we had before treatment. One patient, on preparing to leave, said, "Is this all? Will I never be anything more? Am I doomed always to be just me, with all my failures and my inconsistencies?" She was not thinking at the moment of how much she had changed, of how her allergies had disappeared, of how she had been able to make a satisfactory marriage and become well established in her career. According to Freud, every analysis is incomplete. Accepting that we are imperfect beings is part of taming our grandiosity. We must do that in analysis, too; we must settle for an imperfect analysis.

Often a panic can be averted at this point if the analyst has warned the patient ahead of time to expect the return of symptoms when termination of the analysis is anticipated. The individual who has been forewarned is less likely to feel the treatment has been a failure and better able to find the strength to see through the difficult period ahead.

There is a difference, however, between the original symptom and its return at termination. The presenting symptom was experienced without insight and generally caused great pain and restriction; the new version generally is briefer, less painful, and quickly yields to the insight gained in the treatment. Such a situation indicates that the patient understands the origin of the conflict and is able to clear up the remnants without the help of the analyst. Thus a satisfactory termination acts as a mini-refresher course on the history of the illness. It prepares the soon-to-be ex-patient to handle the return of symptoms, should they reappear after the analysis is over.

One technique I have found helpful in resolving dependencies usually comes into play toward the end of an analysis. The patient will bring up what he or she fears most about ending. Sometimes the fear will come up in a dream. Each fear must be traced to its roots. They almost always relate to some trauma suffered by the patient at a time he or she was too small or powerless to handle it without support.

Was the person left alone at times of emotional transition? Then surely he or she feels abandoned now. One patient dreamed at termination that she had to ascend a huge staircase in which the steps were very far apart, almost too huge for her little legs to span. And she had to climb alone. This woman was reexperiencing her childhood feeling that every step upward was taken without the support of her parents. It is helpful to point out to this kind of person that being frightened or lonely at age three is very different from the aloneness of an emotionally mature individual.

Was the patient abused or sexually molested when no one was around for protection? Rest assured that is precisely what he or she unconsciously fears will happen again when the analyst no longer is available, for in the unconscious mind the patient still sees himself as a little child subject to the mercy of the perpetrator of the crime. Such a person must be made aware that he or she is now an adult who in all likelihood is as physically strong as the analyst.

Was the pain of weaning unbearable for the infant? The adult analysand unconsciously fears that the analytic weaning will be equally painful. The difference must be made clear: The original weaning was initiated prematurely by the mother, while the patient himself has brought up the prospect of leaving and (hopefully) is ready for the termination of the analysis.

Did the patient lose a parent or major person in his life when he was a child? The pain was truly unbearable, and he is afraid he will experience it again. In addition, when a parent dies, the child loses his support and guidance forever, and his life is greatly impoverished by the loss. The patient has to learn that, unlike the child who lost a parent prematurely, the grown-up individual is well able to function on his own or to find others to substitute for the missing analyst.

Whatever the separation anxiety has wrought in a patient

during his lifetime will be reexperienced during termination of the analysis. Each fear must be analyzed and reanalyzed in the safety of the analyst's office until it loses its terror, and the patient can experience it anew without falling apart or resorting to symptoms.

The subject of termination can be brought up by either the patient or the analyst.[2] The earliest analytic treatment, the work of Jose F. Breuer with Anna O., was terminated solely by the analyst. The analysis was an unquestionable failure, in that the patient remained in a sanitarium for a time and never married because of the lifelong bitterness she felt toward men. Conversely, Freud's patient Dora ended her own analysis, without the idea ever having occurred to her analyst. Her treatment also was a failure, in that she became a hypochondriacal complainer for the rest of her life. With the Wolf Man, the analyst also insisted on termination. In this case, however, Freud allowed the patient a year in which to terminate. Nevertheless, many analysts, including the present writer, have questioned whether the recurrent illnesses throughout the life of the Wolf Man could have been avoided had his termination been conducted differently.

Can a termination set for reasons of the analyst's desire to relocate be successful? Here, in contrast to the treatment of the Wolf Man, the termination is set not for reasons of the analyst's dissatisfaction with the patient, but because of the needs of the analyst. This, of course, is a question of great interest to me. According to Maxwell Gittleson[3] who states that the analysis should always be conducted in such a way that it can be interrupted at any point without destroying the patient, the answer is yes. She indicates that it helps to inform the patient of the future plans of the analyst in order to satisfactorily analyze the reactions of the patient to the leave-taking.

In the case of my practice, the situation was somewhat different. As early as five years before my retirement, I decided not to take on new analytic patients. The few patients I accepted for psychotherapy were informed at the start that their treatment would be of short duration. The situation and health of each analytic patient was carefully considered before I finalized my plans. As a result, most of them were able to finish their analyses over the course of the next five years. This did not make it easy for them, but at least in most cases both they and I considered them ready for termination. A few recalcitrant patients were referred to other analysts.

All analysts agree that premature termination, whatever the reason, is highly undesirable. Jack Novick[4] estimates that between 31 and 72 percent of cases reported in the literature terminated prematurely, in that the patient left before the analyst was satisfied that enough work had been done to insure a satisfactory outcome. Ernst A. Ticho's results concurred with Novick's, but noted a difference between patients' and analysts' satisfaction with the outcome of their treatment.[5] Most analysts feel that patients are interested mainly in the alleviation of their symptoms, while the analysts are likely to have more ambitious goals. Gittleson believes that the role of analysis is to help the patient achieve the best possible adaptation. "One must settle for the possible," he states.[6]

The current model for termination is that the patient first brings up the idea, the analyst agrees, and together they analyze the reasons for and the patient's reactions to the prospect. They then set a termination date and analyze the patient's reactions during the termination period. Once the idea of termination has been brought up, it always becomes the focus of the treatment.

The above procedure is the one I follow, along with most of my cohorts. I much prefer that the patient bring up the subject of termination first. Most of us have been weaned, toilet trained, sent to school, and so on when it suited our parents, instead of out of organic needs. For example, one patient was weaned when his mother wanted to go on a trip. Another remembers that her mother said, "Today is the day Janey gives up her bottle!" Both of these patients became procrastinators as adults. In analysis it became clear that they never knew whether an anticipated action grew out of a wish of their own or was something they felt they were supposed to do. When it was the former, it was forbidden; when it was the latter, they balked. When the analyst sets the termination date for such procrastinators, their psychological pattern is repeated. When the patient sets the date and the analyst makes sure the decision has grown out of an organic need, a repetition of the original pathology may be at least partially averted.

The value of the above-mentioned procedure for termination has been tested by various experiments. Hartlaub, Martin, and Rhine[7] collected seventy-one cases and studied the patients' contact with their analysts after termination. The authors concluded that the patients had to continue work that was unfinished in the termination phase. Incomplete achievement included insufficient de-idealization of the analyst, inadequate establishment of the self-analytic function, and only partial integration of achievements into the person's self-image.

Arnold Z. Pfeffer, in a widely quoted, ingenious experiment, originated a method in which follow-up studies of satisfactorily analyzed patients were conducted by a second analyst several years after the termination of analysis.[8] The interviews took place once a week, with the patients in a seated position, and varied in number for different patients from two to seven weeks.

This procedure seemed to elicit the necessary information for an adequate evaluation of the results of analysis. The patients freely discussed the symptoms and problems that had emerged in the course of their earlier activities, as well as their current status. These successfully analyzed patients seemed to revive their analytic transferences as soon as they reentered the office for the follow-up interviews. They spontaneously communicated in a manner reminiscent of free association and, not infrequently, with dreams. The follow-up analyst posed occasional clarifying questions in the context of the material brought by the patient. The patient experienced "brief, transient but vivid recurrences of the analytic transference, including the symptoms for which analysis was first sought." It is particularly significant that patients returned to the last point of the analysis, that is, termination, and relived the separation. This could not be thoroughly analyzed at the time, because the patient had left analysis, even though the meaning of termination may have been partially analyzed before the patient left treatment.

What appeared is a two-step regression, first to the image of the treating analyst and the associated conflicts mastered in the transference as shown by substitution of analysts; and second, regression beyond the treating analyst to "significant infantile figures, conflicts, and their related symptoms." The image the patient retains of the treating analyst is displaced onto the follow-up analyst with all the distortion of the original transference.

On the basis of his observations, Arnold Pfeffer concludes that after an analysis is completed, both the transference neurosis and its resolution continue to be mentally represented and remembered. Therefore they were repeated in the follow-up study as well as in life. He states, "Memories of these analytic experiences are organized around the person of the analyst and play an important role in coping with life situations in less neurotic and more adaptive ways." But instead of a neurotic repetition of the infantile conflict in the follow-up, the former patient now experiences only a mini-version of the original neurosis, which culminates in the same solution reached during treatment. In the analysis of neurosis, conflicts are not shattered but lose their poignancy. While the neurotic person repeats his patterns without insight, the successfully analyzed person in new situations that require mastery repeats briefly and with less intensity the conflicts of the past. Then he resolves them with the solutions gained in analysis.

The follow-up study, in the context of a revived transference neurosis as well as the quick subsiding of symptoms, appears to support the idea that conflicts and underlying symptoms are not actually obliterated by analysis but are simply better mastered with new and more adequate solutions.

Dr. Pfeffer then concludes that the reappearance of hitherto resolved conflicts is not in itself an indication for further analysis. On the contrary, he sees this type of repetition as an achievement of the analysis. It implies the capacity to regress under the services of the ego, to charge new situations with psychic energy, and to manage and master them. He further concludes that if the successfully analyzed patient is capable of doing this in the new setting of a follow-up study, he also is able to use his newfound abilities to master situations in life.

Pfeffer's findings are in keeping with Freud's conclusions in "Analysis Terminable and Interminable," where he states,[9]

[By] a permanent settlement of an instinctual demand [we] certainly do not mean that we cause the demand to disappear, so that it never makes itself felt again. As a rule this is impossible and not even desirable. No, we mean something else, something which may be roughly described as the "taming" of the instinct. That is to say, it is brought into harmony with the ego . . . any solution of an instinctual conflict holds good only for a particular strength of instinct, of the ego, or rather where there is a particular relation between the strength of an instinct and the strength of the ego. If the latter becomes enfeebled, whether through illness, exhaustion or for similar cause, all the instincts which have so far been successfully tamed may renew their demands and strive in abnormal ways after substitutive satisfactions. We have irrefutable proof of this statement in what takes place in dreams, when the reaction to the ego's condition in sleep is the awakening of instinctual demands.

In another study, Arnold Pfeffer discovered that there is a marked tendency among analysts to underestimate the results of their work. In his opinion, the analyst often has a tendency to regard results with "excessive skepticism and to underestimate them . . . [this] was especially evident in those cases where the analytic and therapeutic results were good. In some cases it appeared that the analyst had a certain mental set toward the patient, namely that of the analyst 'analyzing,' which involves having a 'sharp eye' for pathology, emphasizing the conflicts presenting themselves and being relatively unconcerned about the conflicts solved. In a sense, while analyzing, the analyst 'looks for trouble,' and properly so . . . however it appears that this . . . attitude . . . while valuable in the course of analysis, tends to color objectivity in making overall evaluations, in the direction of underestimating results. . . . It seems that an 'outside' analyst is able to add an extra note of objectivity to the treating analyst's evaluation of results."[10]

Later Dr. Pfeffer came to believe that patients bring up the idea of termination after five or six months of feeling well. Therefore he postulated that awareness of positive affect is one criterion of readiness for termination.[11]

S. Firestein's review of the literature on termination[12] deals with criteria for terminating psychoanalytic treatment. Among other indications, he lists symptomatic improvement, change in the structure of the personality as indicated by genetic insight, better object relations, a strengthened ego, and the ability to distinguish more sharply between fantasy and reality. He found symptomatic improvement to be an unreliable standard unless it is supplemented by insight into the roots of the conflict.

In *Dream Portrait* we established the following criteria for what we call the pretermination phase of analysis. These criteria, which are used to determine that the patient is psychologically prepared for termination, include such changes as improved reality testing, better tolerance of anxiety, shame, and depression with diminishing ego defenses, openness in dealing with conflict-laden material, increase in distance from parental figures, increased self-awareness, the ability to take on the role of the analyst, and qualitative and quantitative changes in functioning.[13]

Ernst A. Ticho makes a clinical distinction between treatment goals and life goals.[14] He defines life goals as those the patient would seek if he could put his potentialities to use. They are divided into professional and personal goals. Professional life goals refer to achievements in one's chosen work. Personal life goals refer to the kind of human being one would like to be.

Treatment goals consist of removal of obstacles to the patient's discovery of his potentialities. The latter are greatly dependent upon the uniqueness of the patient's personality, and include the establishment of mature personal relationships and the diminution of narcissistic self-centeredness, freer approach to the unconscious, and a more tolerant, integrated superego. There should also be freer access to the infantile mainsprings of love and hate as well as infantile dependency needs. The patient must achieve not only a good knowledge of his limitations but also the capacity to endure a certain amount of anxiety, suffering, and depression.

Among the possible indicators of readiness for termination that appear before the patient is prepared to actually propose leaving treatment are the elimination of symptoms and reports of changes in relating to others as reported by the patient's friends or family. Changes illuminated by the analysis of dreams, jokes, and screen memories (ostensible recollections, which are really a cover for more significant occurrences) are also useful in predicting the approaching termination.

According to J. Cavenar and J. Nash, it is commonplace to receive "typical termination dreams" after the decision to end treatment has been made.[15] They state that these dreams are the patient's manner of informing himself and the analyst that his conflicts have been worked through and he is ready for termination. R. Gillman states that among dreams reported in the termination phase proper are those suggesting equality with the analyst, such as sharing activities, having lunch together, and being classmates.[16] Other such dreams deal with sadness and resignation.

My patients have presented many termination dreams during the course of their analyses. Frequently these have consisted of such dreams as sailing off alone into uncharted waters, overcoming monumental obstacles, climbing previously unscaled heights, or buying a new house. One man dreamed that he was swimming deep in the ocean and didn't need to breathe. The dream was very pleasurable, and he concluded that he felt as self-sufficient as he must have felt in the womb.

Martin S. Bergmann spoke of the communicative function of dreams and stated that when impending termination is communicated by a dream, it is an indication of inner conflict.[17] Otherwise it would be unnecessary for the idea to appear in a dream. The struggle consists of the thought of leaving the analyst and the analysis, encompassing both the wish to leave and the fear of loss. Both are present to some degree in all patients who contemplate ending their analyses. But the conflict must be resolved before a patient is ready for termination.

H. Gaskill uses realistic thinking as the criterion of the analytic progress.[18] Acceptance of the incompleteness of every analysis is a corollary. The patient must accept what cannot be altered as well as what has been changed. Leon Grinberg stresses the significance of allowing the analysand to have goals that are different from the analyst.[19] He adds that it is important to the analyst to mourn the loss of his omnipotence and to accept the impossibility of resolving all the problems he sees in the patient. Ernst A. Ticho concurs by emphasizing that analysts must master their therapeutic ambition.[20]

Jerome Oremland sees the termination phase as a test of previous analytic work.[21] According to him, dreams in which the analyst appears undisguised portend a good result.

Perhaps the most important development in a successful analysis concerns the emotional assimilation of the analyst by the patient. He is able to take inside himself the image of a kindly, understanding, helpful, objective analyst, who is usually the opposite of the all-too-fallible parents many of us have suffered under. When this process is successful, the actual presence of the analyst becomes extraneous, for the patient has his own inner replica of the analyst to take out whenever he feels the necessity. For example, John Jones, the young man discussed in *Dream Portrait,* had a dream toward the end of his analysis. In it, he was walking along the beach by the water. Everywhere John went, the moon followed alongside. "You are like the moon, the constant moon," John said. "Wherever I go, I know that you will follow along with me." John was no longer dependent on the physical presence of the analyst and was able to terminate his analysis shortly thereafter.

I like to see my patients able to take over the role of the analyst in other ways, too. If all has gone well, the analyst inside of them will say what they thought he or she would feel, for example, "Well done!" or "You felt like this before, and it worked out fine." Most important of all, the former patient should be able to take on the analyst's job of looking at himself analytically, especially his or her own dreams. This usually happens so smoothly that the ex-patient is no longer aware that the thought originally came from his analyst. If the process has occurred as it should (and what we call internalization has taken place), the therapy has never really ended, and growth will continue for life.

This conviction is corroborated by G. Blanck and R. Blanck, who state that termination is appropriate when the functions of the object (analyst) are performed by the self so that the absence of the object becomes tolerable.[22] If the person formerly needed by the patient to regulate self-esteem has been replaced by an internally reliable image, the dream may provide a clue to readiness for termination. Termination means the acceptance of the metaphorical death of the analyst. This prepares the patient to live with the actual as well as the psychological death of his parents.

By the end of an analysis the patient should feel free during the sessions to say anything that comes to mind, no matter how embarrassing, unimportant, or painful. It is highly desirable that the former analysand find a mate or a close friend with whom he or she may experience the same freedom of expression and know that whatever the thought or feeling, it is simply more human than otherwise. It is especially important to be able to express anger or annoyance to one's friend; otherwise it mounts up inside like steam, which does not always find a satisfactory outlet before exploding.

It is essential that a healthy person be able to express gratitude and feelings of love to the analyst before termination can occur. After all, theirs has been the most intimate relationship of which human beings are capable. Together they have come through love, loss, pain, terror, hate, guilt, shame, fear, horror, and the recapturing of childhood bliss and disappointment. They have experienced jointly the most primitive material the patient has ever known. They have relived many childhood traumas and set them to rest. They have gone on a fascinating journey together through the strange underworld of the unconscious. If the patient is not able to express gratitude and love at this point, it suggests that feelings of envy and hostility have not yet been worked through, and that person is not yet ready for termination.

Unfortunately, wishes do not always come true, even for the best-analyzed people! It is helpful to our emotional balance to have some portion of our lives, no matter how small, where things can be as we wish them. Artists and writers are fortunate in this respect. They are free to create their own worlds according to their desires. Perhaps this is why so many people strive for the creative life, despite its practical disadvantages. Other professions sometimes have this possibility built into the work situation. For example, one patient who was the head of his department at a university set about to "build his own empire." Another patient, a failed actor, enthralled a small section of the world by becoming a successful lecturer. It used to be said that "a man's home is his castle." This still should be true to some extent for women as well as men. Then we each will own a spot on earth where we make our dreams come true.

Do you want more than this? Sometimes it is possible to have it. A well-analyzed person should not be conscience ridden or stuck in the realities of daily life to the exclusion of investigating his or her deepest wishes.

Thoreau renounced civilization as he knew it to live alone at Walden Pond. It brought him the peace of mind he valued above all else. Gauguin gave up his family and the security of being a successful stockbroker to follow his destiny to Tahiti. His courage allowed him to live out his destiny as a great artist. Similarly Somerset Maugham left his career as a physician to become a highly successful author.

On the other hand, an untalented house painter would be foolish to traipse off to Tahiti to become another Gauguin. Analysis also should give us the capacity to relinquish the impossible, as well as to go after the possible dream. And most important of all, it should give us the ability to know the difference between the two.

As previously stated, there is sometimes a discrepancy between the goals of treatment and of life. Unfortunately, life's goals cannot always be met. And sometimes the aims of treatment can be satisfactorily achieved, and the person still not be happy. One patient had a retarded son, whom she was bringing up alone. The boy was extremely difficult, as he had no one else in his life, and clung to his mother with all his might. Although she learned to cope with him better, to take advantage of hired help as much as possible, and to find other areas of gratification in her life, it is understandable that she did not leave analysis a satisfied woman. She wanted analysis to cure her son and, of course, it was impossible.

Another woman desperately wanted to marry. Although she was well aware of the dynamics of her case, either she had been too damaged in her youth to relate well to another person, or it is too difficult for some women of a certain age to find a mate. She blamed the analysis for this failure of hers and left treatment angry with the analyst.

Similarly, there is a difference between giving up the analyst as a professional and giving him up in real life. Whatever his attempts at neutrality, the analyst has been there for the patient for many years, has accepted his love, hatred, selfishness, grief, pettiness, and vindictiveness, and seen his inner beauty as no one ever has before. The analyst has stuck with him through sickness and health, through sessions of discouragement and hours of joy, through times of personal attack and criticism, through periods of complete silence. The patient has had the absolute attention of the analyst for three to five hours a week for many years. In a way it is an experience that will never come again. Giving up the analyst as a real person cannot be resolved by analysis; as with other forms of bereavement, the loss cannot be fully analyzed; it can only be endured until it heals over. And perhaps not even then.

Some Come Back

A funny thing happened to me on my way to retirement. Old patients came back! For various reasons, a goodly number of those who had heard of my retirement called or wrote for an appointment. It seemed they wanted to touch base with me before they were ready to let go permanently. This was true particularly if there was something about the analysis that was left unfinished or unsettled.

Take the case of Sylva, a young woman of twenty-six who came to me for a weight problem. The first time I saw her she weighed 180 pounds and wore what only could be described as fluffy rompers. She looked to me like a huge toddler. Sylva had had very little mothering in her life, and she tried to make up for it with food. Apparently the nurturing she got from me enabled her to lose 60 pounds and to learn to dress in a very chic manner, so that soon she became quite unrecognizable. Sylva was a very competitive person, and despite the good results of analysis and her pleasure at "getting a whole new body," Sylva was unable to give me (another woman) the satisfaction of knowing how important I had been. So despite all her progress, Sylva left treatment with me and went to a "more powerful" male analyst.

I was never very happy about it, feeling that somehow I had been shortchanged. But as the years went by and the grapevine brought good news about Sylva, gradually I was able to put it to rest. "So be it," I thought. "We could have done a lot worse."

Imagine my surprise ten years later when I received the following letter:

Dear Alma:

When I heard you were planning to retire, I thought I might want to contact you. Then I saw a television program about a therapist, played by Mary Tyler Moore, who was treating a dying woman. I remember you telling me that you went to the hospital for a session, because that's where your patient was. Moore reminded me of you in your courtesy and generosity—two qualities I have difficulty with still. I feel I fall so short of the person you are, even after hundreds of years of treatment.

I'm sorry I had to find you not enough at the time I did. I will never forget your faith in me, and great kindness and warmth, all of which I have only recently begun to fully appreciate.

Love,
Sylva

I invited Sylva to lunch, and it was as if time had left no rupture between us, as if two close friends took up again where we had left off years before. I told her I thought she had left the analysis prematurely and gave her the reason I thought she had. She agreed and asked me for a referral to someone I thought could continue the work we had begun. She was a delight to be with, and I felt proud to have had some input in her growing up. Incidentally, she had retained her svelte appearance.

As we parted, I said to Sylva, "Our meeting completes the picture for me."

"That's funny," she answered. "For me it just opens it up."

Art was a gentle, charismatic professor of music who began analysis with me when he was in his early thirties and then moved to another state. His mother had died when he was eight years old. When he came into treatment, he vaguely remembered her but didn't believe she had loved him and had no feeling for her. We worked for years to make her come alive for him. Then, one day, as he recalled a scene in exquisite detail in which she had knelt lovingly in her garden, she suddenly began to seem real. Then he could perceive that indeed she had loved him very much.

Much of Art's life changed after his new perception of his mother. He experienced less anxiety, got on better with his wife, and developed beautiful friendships with his students whom he could mother as he felt he had been mothered. Shortly after, he accepted a position in another state.

But it seemed that when he relocated, he left his mother behind in my office. The new image of her faded when he was away too long, and some of his old anxiety returned. For twenty years after he moved away, he felt an occasional need to return to find her again.

When he found out I was retiring, he asked for a special session, saying it was urgent that he see me before I left. During the session, he said:

"When I first came to you, I had no emotional memory of my mother at all. And then one day, here in this room, a miracle happened. I found my mother. She was just as real as if she were standing before me, her dark dress, her lined face, her serious look. Yes, I really had a mother. I found her here in this room. And today I can complete the picture. I had to have this final hour. I never said good-bye to my mother. I need to say good-bye to you first; then I can say good-bye to her, too."

A friend of mine had similar experiences with patients who contacted her after their treatment ended. She said, "I've retired so many times I think I'm going to quit trying to quit."

Will that happen to me, too, I wonder?

Frequently the "touching home base" occurs by mail. Recently I received this opus from Marcia, a woman who had successfully completed an analysis undertaken to relieve a debilitating depression:

A View from the Other Side
Reflections on Post-Termination

Anyone currently in psychoanalysis or who knows someone in analysis or who is contemplating being analyzed wonders if it will ever end. If it does, what is it like to leave the relationship that sustained you through years of growth and change? Here are some thoughts by one who recently "crossed to the other side" to join the ranks of the psychoanalyzed.

The first month was one of exhilaration and celebration of growth and autonomy. I felt enormously empowered and eager to continue on my own the rich work that characterized the final months of the analysis, known as the "termination phase." There was a wish to share with the world what had been accomplished by my analyst and me. Of course, I understood that the inner process would continue for a lifetime and that I had merely acquired the knowledge and skills to continue my development, along with my now-internalized analyst-partner. Further, I knew that she would be available in person should I need a consultation or more analytic work.

That first month was also one of liberation—freedom from a rigid schedule of appointments, transportation, systematic recollection of dreams and the between-sessions work needed to move ahead through insight and self-knowledge. But the formal phase was over, and I wondered what I would do with all the free time. It felt dizzying to be released and encouraged to fly solo.

The second month, however, was a letdown, for it went beyond the accustomed vacation from analysis—an August in January, as it were. This time the "vacation" was not going to lead to an anticipated reunion and resumption of the analytic relationship. Instead, dialogues with my analyst were now internal; there were even times when I found myself consulting her in not so *sotto voce*. I bore little resemblance to the mature, integrated person who had bade her farewell at our final, bittersweet session.

While my professional work and friendships were rewarding, I longed for that significant relationship that distinguished itself by its depth and honesty. A profound loss was beginning to be experienced by me; the process of mourning had begun. Occasionally I had to overcome the wish to race to her office, throw myself on the couch, and pick up where we had left off. In my fantasy there would be no need to explain my presence, since our understanding was so finely attuned. Indeed, we had reached a linguistic economy, thanks to the wealth of our shared, tacit knowledge.

Later that month, during a brief bout with the flu, I suffered a fever-induced nightmare which filled me with a terrifying sense of loneliness. I had been abandoned; I was a fraud and, moreover, the analysis had been a failure. By morning I regained my balance and reason. I reviewed the profound visceral and personality changes that had taken place in me during the analytic years. Gone were the crippling backaches, stomach pains, and lack of energy. I had become free to expand my professional life and was now balancing two careers as I gradually eased into the second. Having weathered the trauma of sudden widowhood, it was now possible for me to redefine myself as a single woman. In short, I was comfortable with the person I had become with the help of psychoanalysis. There was a surge of exhilaration as I contemplated the challenges and satisfactions that lay ahead.

I was aware that when one mourns a loved one, a void is created which, in time, will be filled. It became apparent to me that the intense relationship with my analyst would serve as a preparation for other meaningful relationships that would continue to enrich my life.

In the ensuing weeks there have been numerous occasions to test my ability to make use of the strengths acquired in the analysis. Once again, dreams have become important avenues for deeper understanding, and a sense of self-worth now blends with a more benign acceptance of my own frailty as well as others'. I must confess to a curiosity about the effect that my termination of analysis has had on my analyst. While she was many different people to me over the years, I was always a real person to her. And real people miss each other when they part.

With deep love and gratitude always,

Marcia

Marcia asked what effect the patient's termination has on the analyst. Now I can try to answer that question, as I never could have while I was working in analysis. For the analyst must remain a "blank screen" as much as possible, allowing the patient room to project his or her own distortions upon the image of the "real" analyst. But now that my life as an analyst has ended, I no longer see any need to hold on to analytic neutrality. So here, Marcia, is the effect of the patient's termination on one analyst.

I believe it is always painful as well as heartwarming to terminate an analytic case. The deeper and stronger the feelings the patient has for the analyst, the more profound will be the feelings of loss the analyst will experience. Together patient and analyst have gone through many of the most intimate, demanding, painful, joyous, shameful, significant moments it is possible for human beings to share. Together we have felt great hate, great love, pathos, amusement, loss, and grief. If we were lucky, we also have discovered together what Freud called some of the "great truths of human nature." And now the party is over; it is the analyst's loss as well as the patient's. It always hurts to say good-bye to people we love, but usually we know that some-time, someday, they will return. Each termination of analysis is like the death of a loved one in that we must be prepared to say good-bye to someone we never will see again.

It is not only the patients themselves who are lost to retiring analysts. We have seen these people many times over during the course of years. For some of us the span that remains is all too fleeting. We have invested our time, our thoughts, our emo-tions in our patients for many decades. We have given them a most important part of ourselves. When they walk out the door that last time, they take a piece of us with them forever. For regardless of the joys we anticipate, each closing door is the end of an era that will never return.

Imagine, then, what it must be like to terminate an entire practice at the same time, to say good-bye within a week to many people who have been highly significant in one's life. For me it was one of the most excruciating periods I have ever expe-rienced—far more difficult than I could have anticipated. Some analysts say that no one should terminate a practice without returning to therapy oneself. I know what they mean. But for reasons of pride, or perhaps megalomania, or maybe even real-ity, I felt I could handle it myself, with the support of friends and family. And so I did.

Why is it so difficult? First of all, termination probably means that each patient, at least for a while, will appear at his worst, her most neurotic, his most demanding, her most unpleasant. For each one experiences the impending separation as a repe-tition of all previous losses. And each person tends initially to respond in the same nonadaptive way learned as a child, with all the lies and self-deceptions that help human beings accept

unbearable truths. So it is necessary that the terminating analyst help each patient tolerate without symptoms the worst pain
he or she has ever endured. When he can truly fathom the pain
he tried to avoid in the past, he is not so likely to repeat it again.
Freud said, "The person who doesn't remember is doomed to
repeat." We try to help our patients remember the pain they
would rather forget. All this at a time when the analyst is also
in a state of mourning.

What it meant for me as well as my patients was that I, too,
had to recapture the grief experienced at every significant loss
in my life, from birth onward. This included mourning all over
again lost infancy, parents, analyst, children who have left
home, dearly departed friends and lovers, as well as unfulfilled
hopes and dreams. Giving up the work of a lifetime also means
handing over the throne to younger, fresher rivals, who perhaps will succeed in a manner we cannot yet imagine. While
this is what we desire intensely with all of our better selves,
who among us can turn over the throne without feeling at least
a twinge of resentment? Terminating a practice means facing
the fact of aging as well as imminent mortality. For winding up
the work of a lifetime brings us that much closer to death.

How did I handle this? I grieved. For each and every significant patient. At the death of a beloved person, the mourner
must reexperience each important incident they spent together,
in order to integrate the loss. This is called the working-through
process. I had to begin to work through the potential loss of my
practice and my patients. The process ostensibly began with a
dream a year before I officially retired. In the dream I am looking at my checkbook. The entries are all there, but there are no
numbers for the amounts of the checks that I've entered. The
dream informed me that while I knew all the facets of my analytic career, I did not yet know how it all added up. In a few
months I would begin the task of finding out. To do so, it was

necessary to relive the history of each patient in the attempt to understand the course of the treatment. What went well? What went badly? Why? Am I satisfied with the results? Well, good. But what about the patient who died of cancer fifteen years after her treatment was over? Was that my "fault"? Was it triggered by a psychosomatic conflict I didn't understand? If so, could it have been avoided if I had known more? Freud thought not, that certain problems couldn't be stirred up unless they were active at the time. Thus my "working through" continued back to the beginning of my professional career. Could I have done anything more for this person? Should I have referred that one to another analyst? Should I have sought further supervision, or even another analysis? What would I handle differently now? Would I do it all over again if I could? All these questions had to be answered before I could finish mourning my lost career. The process, like grieving over a death of a loved one, took well over a year. Only then could I truly retire and get on with the rest of my life.

A curious phenomenon occurred a few months after I actually retired that helped me with this process. The patients weren't the only ones who had to "come back" to analysis; to my surprise I found that I did, too. Just as some of them had to return to me to conclude the work of their analyses, I had to come back to some of them to complete matters that had left me dissatisfied. But the avenue that was open to patients to "finish up" by reopening contact was not available to me. First of all, it is extremely important that patients find out that their analysts will let them go. For some people, this is the only experience of its kind they will ever know. In addition, I do not believe it is wise to interfere with the manner in which patients choose to deal with the loss of their analyst. This provided a dilemma for me; I needed to "drop the other shoe" of my career of forty years, but the only people who could supply the "shoe" were not available. So I took the only route open to me; I began dreaming about those patients with whom I had unfinished business.

An example is the case of Marilyn Moyers, a young woman who had been terribly disappointed in the results of her analysis. While the analysis itself seemed to proceed quite well, and she gained much insight into the causes of her illness, she never achieved the life goals she had set for herself. She wanted to be an actress, and after one successful part on Broadway when she was very young, had never really worked professionally again. She had made a good compromise in the opening of a school of acting, which was quite successful. She was a talented teacher and earned an excellent living. But she never was able to accept her "failure" in a business where perhaps 2 percent of the members of Actors' Equity make an adequate living at their trade. As a result, she blamed the analysis. If she had gone to a better analyst, she reasoned, it would have made her successful in her chosen career. Interpretations as to what success meant to her on an unconscious level were rejected with contempt, and she left the analysis furious with analysis and me. I was not happy about the manner in which her analysis ended and felt that Marilyn was right in her criticism to the extent that her problem never really had been resolved. Whether another analyst could have helped her achieve success in the theater, I'll never know. But I regretted that I could not help her attain her desired life goals. I also understood that she was succeeding in frustrating my therapeutic ambitions just as her own were thwarted. It was very painful, just as she meant it to be. She wanted to show me how it felt to fail. And, like Marilyn herself, there was nothing I could do but bear it.

One night while I was working on the mourning process, I went to sleep thinking about Marilyn and worrying that I had failed her. I had the following dream, which literally seemed to go on all night.

Marilyn has come back to analysis for a month or so. She has grown. I look up at her and am surprised to see she is much taller than I am. I feel good about it. Unlike her usual habit, she is wearing high heels. During the long night, somehow I have come to terms with the fact that in addition to anger there are many warm feelings between us. We have shared many profound experiences together, and at times in her treatment we have cared deeply about each other. In real life I seemed to have forgotten this as much as she, as feelings of frustration took over. After the dream I felt much better about her analysis because I realized that our anger toward each other was not the whole story. In the dream I tell her she needs analysis to bring the two kinds of feelings together, that if she allows them to merge, her love for me eventually will temper her hate and disappointment. She is smiling and agrees.

The fact that Marilyn has grown taller in the dream suggests that her own shortcomings—for example, the fact that she never dressed properly when looking for a job—have contributed to the lack of success in her chosen field. She has a self-destructive streak, which showed in her life as well as in the analysis. While she wants me to feel guilty about her failed ambitions, the dream indicates that she herself has further growing to do. Since every dream is a wish, we have to inquire further what my wish is. The high heels she is wearing suggest that I have given her the power and status she really wants. The dream wish also is that Marilyn "grow taller" than I, that she become able to continue the work beyond the point to which the analysis has brought her. I would like her to achieve the insight my disturbed sleep has brought me this night—that she really cares for me as well as wanting to spite me. That will help her accept the reality that we can't get everything we want in life. In my experience half a loaf has it all over starvation.

I can't answer for Marilyn, but somehow the dream work of the night solved my anxiety about her analysis. It also taught me to forgive her for thwarting my therapeutic ambitions. I can't have everything I want in life, either, including curing all my patients. I also know that I did the best I could, and that while the analysis gave her neither the career of her choice nor power and status, it was not an absolute failure. So I finally put to rest the case of Marilyn Moyers. Then I too could sleep.

In another dream of this working-through period, I am in bed with a patient, who is an analyst, and an unknown man. The patient moves over to the center of the bed so that there is very little room for me. I begin to sob, saying, "I know there is no room for me in this bed, and I mean that psychologically. So I have to leave." The patient, who is probably my most talented disciple, says, "No, you *don't* know. Like a fungus growing on the outer edge of a white casserole dish, you don't know that you were put here, or why you were put here. You don't know the whole story." I wake up in profound shock and almost forget the dream.

This patient will take over my career where I leave off. It is the oedipal situation in reverse. Now is the time for me to "give up the throne," difficult as that may be. Just as every little girl must accept that her mother is queen of the household if she is to grow up a healthy, realistic woman, so my juniors in the profession have accepted my reign. Now, however, it is time to turn it over to them. It is psychologically correct, it is the right time, it is the only thing to do unless I choose to become a disgruntled, irritating old woman. As the dream says, there no longer is any "room for me in the bed." But it makes me terribly sad. For I am afraid it signals the end of a meaningful life. I feel as useless as the fungus on the edge of the casserole. But the wise young analyst brings hope. She says I am here for a purpose, a purpose I do not yet understand.

I suddenly am choked up with feeling for what I have known in my head: My life will not be over, for there is much I have yet to accomplish. For example, there are many books in my head that have to be written. It's true I don't know the whole story and, indeed, may never know it. But I trust my unconscious mind, which says I truly am here for a purpose. And the new purpose of my life may well be writing.

In another dream during the same period, I am riding in the back seat of a car making a long journey with my former patient, Marjorie Mars, and her first husband, Larry. He is driving. He is very silent. She is asleep. He doesn't say a word until I begin to eat a bran muffin. I ask him if he is hungry, and he says he is and begins to eat. He then begins to talk, and talks his head off.

Marjorie is the patient I discussed in another chapter. Her analysis took place many years ago, and we have managed to remain lifelong friends. It is true that we have made a long journey through life together, and in many ways our paths have continued to overlap.

She divorced Larry shortly after her analysis ended. Although she has had a wonderful, successful life in many ways, including a second marriage, I suppose I am questioning whether her marriage to Larry could have been saved. Perhaps she and I were "asleep" to its possibilities. For after I "feed" Larry in the dream, he opens up and begins to talk.

The dream has a personal meaning for me, as well. I think of my father, who often was a remote and silent man. I always knew that he loved me but felt he wasn't interested in what I had to say. So I allowed him to remain withdrawn and out of contact with me. To spare myself pain, I think I withdrew from him, too. If I had "fed" him as I did Larry in the dream, if I had given him more, perhaps he would have opened up and become the father I needed. The movie title *I Never Sang for My Father* flashes through my mind. I realize I never took the opportunity to talk to my father about himself, to ask about his background, his parents, his hopes, and his dreams. Now it is too late. I suddenly find myself sobbing.

In the next dream scene, I am with Marcia in a basement apartment. We are in the process of leaving. I tell her that Marjorie is my friend. She says she knows her and likes her very much. In real life, Marcia wants to be my friend too. She and I have much in common, and I could easily imagine her as my friend. I have carefully considered the possibility, but have questioned whether it would be the best thing for her.

Can a friendship between patient and analyst ever take place after the analysis is over? I think the answer usually is no, because of the possibility of interfering with the work of the post-analytic phase.

In addition, many of us are much better people behind the patients' couch than we are with our families and friends. We are all human beings, with our conceits, idiosyncrasies, and foibles, just like everyone else. Total involvement was what the patient needed from his mother when he was an infant and in all likelihood did not get, or he wouldn't be in analysis now. This is what he gets during his time on the couch, and it helps to make up for his earlier deprivation. But it is far easier for an analyst to remain patient, neutral, and wise for forty-five or fifty minutes at a time than for a lifetime, if indeed that would be possible or desirable. While there are certain cases where analysts in training and their former patients have become colleagues and friends, in my opinion it usually interferes with the internalization of the analyst. The image of the good enough analyst must be incorporated as a part of the personality of the ex-patient before he gets his full benefit from the analysis.

Then, too, it is said that no one ever is really able to grow up until the death of his parents. So long as they live, he is still psychologically their child. I think the same state of affairs exists between patient and analyst. The patient must really let go of the actual analyst, before the internalization process is complete.

Let me give a personal example. My five-year analysis was a tremendous success, both in my opinion and that of my analyst. She was warm, insightful, kind, considerate, interested in me, and a wonderful role model of a successful professional woman, wife, and mother. She opened avenues of insight into myself that I had never experienced, and my life was smoother, less conflicted, and more gratifying than it had ever been before. I left analysis feeling deep love and gratitude for her, as well as with an ability to express anger with her when it was called for. My admiration made the termination process both easy and difficult. Easy because I had such good feelings about her and difficult because I had to renounce this lovely woman who had given me more than any other person I'd ever known.

She was the president of an organization of fine, highly trained analysts who invited me to join them at the end of my analysis. I was flattered to be considered for membership and became affiliated with the society as soon as possible. Then the difficulties began. I soon found out that she was at her best as an analyst and that a side of her came out during the meetings that I had never seen before. There she appeared as a dominating, manipulative woman, who ran the organization with an iron fist. During my analysis she had given me the freedom to say and feel what I wanted. But within the analytic circle, she dictated to a clique of members exactly how it should be run, including whom and what to vote for. Perhaps I was politically naive, but it shocked me that the slate of officers and matters of extreme importance really were decided in advance of the elections by my former analyst. The vote was merely a formality. It impressed me as a totalitarian organization not much different in structure from Nazism or Communism. I found the situation intolerable and knew it was impossible for me to remain her puppet. I soon left the association, taking a group of six other analysts with me.

All in all, I think it would have been much better for me to have left the analysis feeling respect as well as love for her, in which case the trauma of our postanalytic relationship might never have occurred.

One does not always heed one's own advice, however, no matter how valuable it may be. I myself have one good friend who was a former patient. This woman, who had known no mothering to speak of in her childhood, went through a long and arduous analysis in which she feels I actually was her mother. She believes that the relationship went far beyond the usual analysis, in which the patient ordinarily recovers memories of good mothering. This woman had few if any such memories to retrieve and feels that her entire new personality is based on her relationship with me. When she left treatment, she wanted to be friends and felt she could do it without any detrimental effects on her development. I agreed, but insisted first on waiting a period of at least a year to see how she managed without me. When it became apparent that indeed she was doing fine, we began to meet now and then for lunch. These meetings have continued for many years, and I believe we made the shift without causing any untoward difficulties for her. But this is an unusual woman with an atypical background. And by and large I still feel it is better for patient and analyst to go their separate ways after the analysis is over.

But despite all my rationalizations, I suppose that the dream about the meeting of Marjorie and Marcia is telling me something. The friendship has worked out well with Marjorie; perhaps, the dream says, it could do the same with Marcia. We shall see . . .

Anyway, Marcia, I hope that this chapter answers your question about the effect of patients' termination on the analyst. But I sincerely doubt that it does. I suspect that what you really wanted to say all along, but didn't quite have the courage to, was, "I miss you. Do you miss me, too?" The answer to your question, Marcia, is an unequivocal yes.

4

Perceiving the Analyst as a Role Model

This is the story of a woman who desperately and courageously fought for her life against the mighty self-destructive forces within her. Because she hated her mother, there was no adult woman in her life whom she could emulate, who could teach her what it was like to be a woman. Hence during her analysis, she developed an overwhelming obsession to possess me thoroughly so that I would always be available to serve as a blueprint for life. Until that happened in a psychological sense, Marjorie would remain a lost and frightened child, with nowhere to go, nothing that interested her, and no role in life she wanted to play except that of a beloved infant.

Marjorie came to me for analysis when she was thirty-five years old. She came ostensibly because she had been doing a "self-analysis," the results of which had so inundated her with terror that she felt forced to find professional help. During the course of her intense self-exploration, she had developed, among other things, a rat phobia and many suicidal thoughts—such as driving her car off a bridge. She also wanted analysis to help her "be less afraid of everything" and "to feel better" (less irritable, hostile, and "mean") about her children.

Her method of selecting a therapist is interesting for the light it casts on her personality. Marjorie asked a friend, whose two children had completed therapy with me, for a referral for her son. Then, rather than admit her need for help to her friend, she came to see me herself.

Marjorie looked like an older version of the typical American college girl. She was rather pretty, of medium height, somewhat slender. The impression she gave was of the average WASP, the well-bred norm one often finds in the commuter towns of Connecticut. She had good but pedestrian features and a quiet subdued manner in speech and dress. It seemed to me that the indistinct impression she made on others reflected her feelings about herself.

"I'm not a person—I never have been. I'm just a collection of agreements designed to circumvent trouble," she said without feeling. It made a great deal of sense to me that this woman who didn't know who she was, this unconnected "collection of agreements" should desperately seek a role model in order to find out how to live her life.

There was an air of simplicity about her, but it was a deceptive one. After careful observation, one was struck by the combination of the childlike and the aging in this woman. For instance, her hair was kept in an outmoded Buster Brown cut, appropriate when she was a child but now the color of it was gray. She had a juvenile air about her but looked tired and worn beyond her years.

This, too, had an emotional correlate; Marjorie recently had become aware of the discrepancy between her psychological and chronological ages. She characteristically wore an expression that impressed this observer as being both poignant and anachronistic in an adult her age. With a wistful gaze, she seemed to be saying, "I'm just a little girl, harmless and innocent. I don't want to hurt you. Don't be mad at me." Her self-image was that of a small girl who cannot afford to antagonize the significant adults in her life. For example, she met a woman at a class meeting who was handling her child somewhat punitively. Instead of the more usual adult response of anger with the mother, Marjorie saw herself as the abused child. "Nobody would want to be that mother's little girl," she remarked. As the analysis proceeded, it became increasingly clear to both of us that Marjorie simply didn't know what it was like to be an adult woman.

Marjorie is a highly intelligent college graduate and a talented graphic artist. Working only a few hours weekly, she earned enough to pay for her treatment. Nevertheless, she impressed the analyst as being shallow and brittle, as though only her intellect was at work; the rest of her personality was sealed off and unavailable to her. Although brilliant and talented, she did not possess the rich and deep personality that was her birthright. The superficial impression lasted until she learned that in analysis it was safe to say whatever came into her mind.

At the time, she had been married for twelve years and was the mother of a girl of seven and a boy of four. Neurotically dependent on her husband, she had played a subservient self-effacing role in the marriage for years, in which she was unable to express the slightest wish or antagonistic feeling of her own. At the same time he had to be handled like a spoiled child, or he would throw a temper tantrum. Marjorie felt she had three children instead of two. This became even more clear to her when she dreamed that her husband was dressed in a pair of little-boy shorts. Obviously, there was no mature husband-wife relationship to threaten her. As one would predict, she was completely disinterested in sex.

Marjorie's relationship with her son also was a difficult one. "I often hate him and treat him meanly," she commented. During the course of her therapy, when she had learned to be more outspoken in her relationship with her husband, Marjorie discovered that she had been using the child as a scapegoat, that because she did not dare risk being angry with her husband, she had been taking it out on the boy. When this insight served to change Marjorie's attitude, her son was able to make important emotional progress, and no longer was considered a problem child. She did not continue to feel that he required therapy. I was moved many years later when I met the now grown-up young man at a party. At that time he thanked me for what I had done for him.

Marjorie is the older of two daughters from a small midwestern town. According to her, and indeed the appraisal was confirmed in analysis, her mother was an icy, unfeeling woman who gave as little of herself as possible to the child.

"Mother never thought I was worth very much," Marjorie cried. "She wasn't really interested in me at all. She took care of me physically because it was her duty. But she never, never touched me unless she had to," she maintained through her sobs, "and then she would be apt to pull away. Would you believe that when she washed me in the bath she would wrap a wash rag around my wrist and hold on to me that way? She really didn't like me, had no time for me, and never even tried to disguise her true feelings. She would see that I was properly fed and dressed because she had to, and then would say, 'Don't bother me. Go out and play.' Then she would lock the front door until dinner time and might simply go and stare out the window."

Marjorie recalls that in her mother's house there was a time for eating, a time for sleeping, and a time for elimination. In all three particulars, Marjorie was placed at the appropriate spot and expected to remain there until the proper response occurred. If it didn't, she had to stay in place until it did. In a similar manner, any suggestion that the rigid scheduling be altered was greeted with surprise, as though the speaker were a bit peculiar. Once Marjorie braved her mother's displeasure by announcing she would like something to eat at a hitherto unreserved-for-food hour. "What do you mean you're hungry?" her mother responded. "It's only three o'clock!"

Marjorie had been breast-fed for a short while but was abruptly weaned when her mother became ill. It seems that the nursing situation was highly eroticized for the mother and that the only physical gratification she ever was able to give Marjorie was a period of total indulgence in very early infancy. At five months, the sudden weaning apparently was experienced by the grieving infant as an ousting from "paradise." She then passed hours of terror in which she waited interminably for an inconsistent mother who appeared only when it suited her. The child was then sent to her maternal grandmother's house for the first of a series of extended visits. The mother never again became available for Marjorie, who shortly thereafter became an overconforming, repressed child whose energies were tied up in wooing an unobtainable mother. Marjorie was a persistent thumb sucker until she reached the age of eight, to the despair of her parents. She still is a nail biter.

She was toilet trained quite young and remembers the entire matter of toilet habits being treated with a combination of interest in every minute detail plus a disgust with the whole business. In fact she felt her mother regarded her daughter's body with the feelings of repugnance she normally reserved for the products of elimination. "One day I caught my mother looking at me naked with a look of bewilderment, disgust, and disappointment," she confides. Naturally enough, Marjorie was not very happy with her body either, to the point where she cannot say the word *breast* without great embarrassment. Several of her statements about her mother indicate that in all likelihood the older woman never accepted her own feminine role at all. Whenever she began menstruating, she would go to bed for the day. It is interesting that the mother's nickname was a boy's name and that her favorite daughter was called "Bobby." Marjorie's mother dressed and undressed behind closed doors, and Marjorie said she never once saw her mother naked. It does not seem strange that such a woman would reject her daughter's femininity, along with her own.

Marjorie says, "My mother never was satisfied with the way I looked. Something was always crooked or loose. She fussed this way and that, but my clothes were never right. And if I liked something, it was always too expensive to buy."

Since one's mother serves as the major role model for a girl's later behavior as a mothering person, it is not surprising that Marjorie came to analysis because of difficulty in handling her own child.

Marjorie's mother was an extremely independent woman. If she needed a pair of curtains and found the exact kind she wanted, she would never buy them. Instead she would purchase the identical material at the same price as the curtains and go home and make her own. According to her daughter, no matter how good the article was, her mother always felt she could make it better herself. "Apparently, I take after her in this respect," Marjorie said. And indeed, it was true. Marjorie had tried to be her own analyst for years and only sought out a professional when she got into terrible trouble.

For most of Marjorie's childhood, her family was well-off financially, and she was taken care of by a constantly changing stream of servants. Her father was first a salesman and later became a minister. "First he sold products," she said, "and then he sold God." His wife frequently accompanied him on his trips for as long as three weeks and left the children behind. Poignantly Marjorie recalled that her mother believed she should never bring back for the children any gifts from these trips. "Children should be glad to see their parents for themselves and not for any presents," she proclaimed.

Marjorie's father had a nervous breakdown sometime during his daughter's early years, and it was at this point that he changed his occupation. As a salesman, he was away from home a good deal, to Marjorie's regret. She greatly preferred her father to her mother and believes she was his favorite as well. "Because I looked like him," she explained. He seems to have been kinder and somewhat more accessible than her mother, who completely subjugated him.

Marjorie remembers her mother completely monopolizing her father on his brief stays at home and believes she made every effort to keep father and daughter apart. As a result of her domination, he seems to have been ineffectual as a parent and relatively unimportant in Marjorie's life. He was more affectionate than his wife, but Marjorie feels his advances always had an ulterior motive, such as to get her to do some work around the house. According to her, "Cleaning up a mess was highly prized because it saved them trouble, but if after considerable effort I learned to jump rope on one foot, it was met with complete indifference." They were interested in themselves and not in her. As a tragic aftermath, Marjorie felt this was true of everyone, even her analyst.

The family moved about a good deal during her childhood, as the father changed his jobs. When the analyst moved her office, Marjorie became extremely upset, enough to cancel her session for the first time. Then memories of childhood moves were recovered, when her family had "no room" to take along her treasured toys. Precious favorites were lost forever. A beloved teddy bear was left behind; a prized bicycle was given away.

Marjorie recalled feeling panic stricken at every move, fearing the family would leave her behind too. When she got older and the family was preparing for another move, she insisted on having her own alarm clock, which she would set for five o'clock, and then remain sleepless all night long to make sure the alarm went off. She was determined not to be left behind.

In the same way, her love for the analyst was anxiety provoking. "Loving you is dangerous," she said. "It gives you the power to walk off and leave me." It was pointed out to Marjorie that what she loved she had always lost.

Marjorie's conflict between dependence and independence began when she was quite young. Growing up was frightening for her because once she had mastered a new skill, there never was any turning back. Even learning to dress herself was not without its struggles. If she put on her own clothes, it was valued "because it saved my mother the bother." But once she learned to do it herself, she was left to dress alone. "Once I learned to tie my own shoelaces, she never tied them again," Marjorie said sadly. Thus she lost even the small degree of attention she had received from her mother. There was no in-between—no loving mother helping a child to dress. Either the mother dressed the child from head to foot "without any nonsense," or the child was left alone to do the job herself. No wonder that emotionally Marjorie had remained a child!

Analysis was fraught with similar dangers in Marjorie's mind; either she did a self-analysis or the therapy would be taken over completely by the analyst. "Like in committee work," she said, "I either did the whole thing myself until I was worn out or I did nothing at all."

Marjorie's father also contributed to his daughter's problems in achieving independence. She recalled that during her adolescence her father began to have financial problems. Things got so bad that when she was in her sophomore year at college, it looked as if she would have to leave school. At that time she was offered a scholarship for "worthy but needy students." Her father got angry at the thought of his daughter "accepting charity" and refused to allow her to take the scholarship. Instead, she was forced to drop out of school for a year, until she could earn enough money to enable her to continue her schooling. She was encouraged by her father to be independent in every way; indeed she was never allowed to indulge an occasional wish for passivity. "Sometimes at home when I just wanted to sit," she reminisced, "he would insist that I get up and do something."

Thus, with both parents constantly proving their independence, the child grew up with no model of genuine autonomy, and had no idea of what it feels like to be an adult.

With this background, it is not surprising that Marjorie wanted from the analyst only the love and gratification that she had missed as a child. She wanted no analysis; that she would do herself. Instead she pleaded for love. It was heartbreaking to watch this adult woman beseech the analyst to pick her up like an infant. At one session she announced, "I had a fantasy about you. I come over to you and unbutton your blouse. I get so scared." She begins to cry. "I just want to be able to come over and touch you and be held close without getting slapped."

The analyst responded, "You want to feel close to me and touch me as you wanted to do with your mother. Only she made you feel it was wrong."

Marjorie was sobbing by now. "That's right," she said. "If I just touched her hand, she would jerk it away as if I really were a rat. Maybe if I was very very still she would let me sit at her feet. But if I even looked at her, she would put me out of the room." She sobs. "I just want to be able to look at you and touch you all at the same time. You know, the past few days I've been looking at people. If I looked at my mother, I couldn't touch her. And if I touched, I couldn't look."

"With me, you want to both look and touch, so you can feel all of a piece," I said.

For years Marjorie continued to interrupt her associations with what she considered analytic interpretations. Her interests tended toward symbolism, with a strong emphasis on breasts and penises, whether they were appropriate or not. Her constant explanations made any depth of feeling and thought all but impossible and contributed to the shallow, brittle impression she continued to give.

Marjorie reacted this way because of a deep fear and mistrust of people, in this case the analyst. She did not trust anyone else to do a good job, to keep her interests at heart, not to harm her. After all, if she gave the "interpretations" herself, she could be sure they were the kind she wanted to hear. As she herself put it, "It's like I'm playing a roulette game with a crooked wheel—it always comes out the way I want it." Then, too, she did not want to be dependent on anyone for fear of being abandoned. I informed her that the patient's job is to say whatever comes to mind, and the analyst's job is to analyze. And that as long as she thought she could do both at the same time, she was fooling herself. Her response was to cry.

She remembers a typical incident that happened when she was seven years old. Her mother had taken her to the hospital, totally unprepared, for a tonsillectomy. Then she left the terror-stricken child alone to be wheeled down the corridor to the operating room. Marjorie remembers with much feeling that she determined never again to depend on the mother who had abandoned her in her time of need. In the future, she vowed, she would rely on no one but herself.

Another significant aspect of the tonsillectomy is that even at the age of seven, she had a deep objection to being anesthetized. She says that when given ether, she jumped down from the table and had to be chased around the room until she was caught. When administered gas by force, a second time, she pretended to be unconscious, in the hope that they would take the mask away. Fortunately or unfortunately, as the case may be, her attempts at deception were unsuccessful. A similar, more mature attempt at deluding the medical profession occurred during her first experience with natural childbirth. When the anesthetist decided that Marjorie required some assistance and proceeded to administer an anesthetic against her will, she announced, "When I get ether I turn blue." Her adult attempts at avoiding unconsciousness met with the same fate as those of the seven-year-old child.

A similar process occurred in her efforts to maintain conscious control in the analysis. If she allowed herself to feel and speak freely, all the fury she had swallowed for thirty years over a cold and rejecting mother might come out against this new mother figure, the analyst. Then Marjorie would be punished, criticized, or abandoned, as she had been before. How much better to control tightly what came out of her. Then perhaps this new mother figure might give Marjorie the love she had yearned for all her life.

Beneath this fear lurked a more frightful one: that to give up control meant vile words might come out of her mouth, or even, horror of horrors, that she might lose control of her excretory functions. Then surely she would be thrown out of the analysis or, at the very least, considered worthless. "If I said whatever came into my mind, everything—my insides—would fall out on the floor. I can see you sweeping it up with a broom, saying 'There goes patient number six-hundred eighty-four,' and throwing me down the toilet." At this point she was able to remember hours of crying and fighting sleep as a child, because to give up consciousness and go to sleep meant she might defecate or urinate and have to pay the consequences.

Still another reason for her fear of losing consciousness was the need to protect herself from harm. In her analysis she could not abandon herself to the process because of her unconscious fear that the analyst would jump out at her and hurt her. During Marjorie's childhood, her mother had a habit of moving stealthily around the house and abruptly striking out at Marjorie (physically as well as verbally) for whatever she happened to be doing. The attacks seemed to have no connection with Marjorie's actions, for what was disregarded one day became an offense on the next. "I never knew when I would be jumped on or why," she lamented.

A significant trait in Marjorie's personality is her strong need to identify with her mother. But because she hates her so, she is determined not to be like her. "When I feel myself wanting to act like my mother," she said, "I try to do just the opposite." For example, her mother always gets dressed behind closed doors, while Marjorie walks around naked. Her mother bought expensive clothes for herself and dressed Marjorie and her sister in made-over flour sacks. Marjorie buys clothes for her children first. In fact, at the time she came into treatment she was the owner of exactly three dresses. Her cold and rejecting mother was determined not to spoil her children. Marjorie makes every effort to be kind to her son and daughter, with no thought of her own needs. It was the failure of the desire to be different from her mother that brought Marjorie into analysis. When she no longer could control the wish to be mean to her son, she got herself into treatment.

A healthy little girl identifies with her mother a great deal, and uses her as a blueprint for how to get along in life. Without a model for guidance, the world does not make sense. Such a child is truly adrift in a morass of confusion. Marjorie allowed herself no such psychological map; hence she not only didn't know who she was but also felt at sea in the adult world.

She didn't want to be like her mother because she hated the

stern, rejecting woman. Yet she desperately craved a mother person she could identify with. If the analyst would only love Marjorie, then she would be able to permit herself to copy her. Apparently she felt loved by me, for she soon began to emulate me with a vengeance.

As a result of her hunger for a role model, she copied my every move for many years. Where I lived, the schools and camps my children attended, even my profession for a brief while, all served as a blueprint to Marjorie of how a woman was expected to behave. Her willingness to use me as a role model was instrumental to her cure and enabled her to function as a wife and mother as she worked in analysis. The identification continued for many years until she found the strength to give me up as a pattern for living and to strike out on her own. It was only then that she could become a whole person with a life of her own as mother, wife, and professional woman.

As stated earlier, Marjorie came to treatment to get rid of her rat phobia and suicidal wishes, to help her be less frightened of everything, and to feel better about her children. After two years of therapy in which she attended sessions five times a week, her symptoms had all but disappeared. The rat phobia and suicidal wishes were apparently the result of misdirected, unconscious rage. In her rat phobia, she could not take the chance of being angry with those she needed, so she "loved" her analyst, her mother, and her husband, and hated and feared the rats. Also, *she* did not feel dirty, worthless, nasty, and ugly, with the urge to bite; it was the rat who personified all these qualities. Her suicidal wishes also represented hateful feelings that she did not dare to express and felt forced to turn back onto herself. "My husband was late in coming home from work," she said. "So I had a fantasy that he drove into the river by accident, and I used the insurance money to come here as much as I wanted."

One evening she came to her session quite elated. "Tonight when I drove by the river," she said, "instead of feeling like driving into it, I had the fantasy of pushing *you* in . . . I suppose you will think that is progress." And indeed I did.

According to Marjorie, she no longer suffers from the compulsive need to please and is proud of her "new selfish personality." It is interesting that Marjorie herself dates her "cure" from the date when she first looked across the street and saw that the trees were round. "Then I realized that all my life I had seen trees and people and everything else as flat, two dimensional, without any depth," she said. "And I never even knew they really looked round. Now I see them the way they are." Then I remembered how her associations had once seemed so flat to me and realized how full and profound they gradually had become without my even noticing the change.

Marjorie left analysis several years later. She divorced her husband and now lives happily with the man she loves. Her children are grown and doing nicely, having presented her with three lovely grandchildren who are devoted to their grandmother. And best of all, she is a full professor and author who teaches one of the humanities at Barnard College.

Shortly after she left treatment, she wrote me the following letter:

Dear Alma:

I feel so different in the last few weeks I can hardly get used to it. I am like a little child who has been yelling his head off for a toy dog, and who didn't even realize he had a dog that was real. I complained and complained how disappointed I was because I couldn't be Marjorie Bond. I didn't know that in a certain sense that's who I really am. I realized this after your first remark, that one day we would talk about my leaving. I expected to burst into tears, but I didn't. I think it was because I know now that I never can really be separated from you. For I have a wonderful filled up feeling that I can take you with me wherever I go.

I was mad at you for so long because you wouldn't give me what I wanted. Now I know that what you did give me was far more important than what I thought I needed. I tried to revive the old nursing fantasies about you. Do you know, I couldn't! I burst into laughter. The picture in my head was me in a baby bonnet. Not so long ago I would have thought that was a nice idea. But now it seems so limited, not what I have in mind for myself at all.

I counter my separation fears, which are relatively mild perhaps, but still being resolved, with the realization that, in another sense, I shall always be indebted to you.

It's not an indebtedness that poses a burden, but springs from my sense of gratitude that you were able to tolerate my weaknesses for so long a time. If you could stand me for so long, I may not be so bad after all. For some time now I have felt very lucky to be getting the things I wanted. Finally I am more often feeling I deserve them.

Possibly, come to think of it, I even deserved getting you. How's that for a new ego?

Love—always—
Marjorie

With all humility, I would like to add that Marjorie Mars is one of my analysands of whom I am most proud.

What Makes Successful Analysis?

Earlier we asked what makes an analysis a success and what accounts for the changes in personality and character structure that lead to a positive outcome. The case history of John Henry Jones provides an excellent study of how and why a personality can be reconstructed by analysis.[1]

John's analysis was highly effective in transforming every important aspect of his life—the ability to understand himself, to love, to hate, to work, to mourn, to allow himself pleasure when appropriate, to maintain a relatively stable mood, to know who he is and be comfortable with it, to see himself and the world realistically, to be independent of his parents and his analyst, to remain emotionally and physically healthy in the face of anxiety and the "slings and arrows of outrageous fortune," and to take over the role of the analyst when his treatment ended.

John was sent to see me by his school counselor, a successfully analyzed former patient of mine, for treatment of his persistent depression. It was a meeting that was to change his life forever. John, a strikingly handsome young man of twenty-four, impressed me as shy, immature, naive, and extremely well mannered and "nice."

It was difficult to tell his response to the interview, as he was very reserved. He also impressed me as quite ordinary and not particularly intelligent or insightful, a misconception that was not to be corrected until late in the treatment when his inhibitions against full intellectual and emotional functioning were removed.

John informed me that he had been born in a small town in Ohio. His mother, the daughter of farmers, had died when he was seventeen years old. His father was a former firefighter. John was a middle child, who had a brother who was four years older and a sister two years younger than he. John always believed he was the favorite of his mother. This fact as well as his striking good looks made him the target of much jealousy from the rest of his family.

His presenting symptom was an unrelenting depression, characterized largely by an inner sense of impoverishment. He had no insight whatsoever as to the cause of his depression. At the time he entered treatment, he had come alone to the big city to enter graduate school. He was the first and only member of his family to leave the town where they were born. John had a dreary existence in New York. He lived by himself, had no friends, and had never had a girlfriend. He would come home from school at night, do his homework, and cry himself to sleep. It was the opinion of the analyst that in addition to missing his family, John had never overcome the loss of his mother and was unable to develop emotionally beyond his age at her death.

John's character structure served as a restraining corset that sifted out all pleasure from his life. Almost any wish, even an innocuous one like buying a sorely needed pair of pants, was put through an emotional wringer. For example, John would attack himself mercilessly with such questions as, Do I really need the pants? Can I afford them? Am I getting my money's worth if I buy them? Are they the kind of pants Dad would approve of? Is the color too bright? Too pale? What about the length? the style? the fit? Are they too feminine looking? and so on. Should need finally drive him to take the plunge after what sometimes were months of obsessing, all conscious pleasure had been wrung out of his purchase. Such was John's way in every aspect of daily living. This was evident from the time he was little, as illustrated by the following remarks:

"I was always such a strict kid. Reminds me of once I couldn't sleep at night. Some surveyors put little red sticks in the ground, to mark off some nearby land. We pulled them out of the ground and made little boats out of them. But at night I couldn't sleep, because we had done this terrible thing. So I told Dad what I did, because I knew I deserved to be punished."

Another time John, a young Boy Scout, was given an assignment to study some rules from the manual. He began to cry because he didn't think he could read the whole book before the next scout meeting. His mother called the scout master and told him John's dilemma. The scout master responded, "Where did he get that idea? I only assigned the first chapter!"

It turned out that John's character structure was a carbon copy of his father's, as indicated in his associations to a dream:

"My boss had a sweater on—like the one Dad used to wear when we worked in the yard. He was always so strict and rigid. We couldn't cut up at all—if we fooled around Dad would holler—He's so . . . serious—he didn't even talk. That could have been a good time for us to talk together or kid around with each other. Why couldn't he enjoy us? 'Get that job done right!' he would yell. 'No nonsense! Clip that bush, rake those leaves, pick the weeds!'

"He was always sitting back waiting for us to make a mistake. Then he would pounce. Passing food at the table, everything had to be passed in the right direction, like in the army. God forbid if you stalled. I sat tight in my seat afraid to move. 'Move your plate closer!' It had to be exactly at the edge of the table. [John begins to laugh.] Meanwhile he always got a spot of spaghetti sauce on his big belly. He hated kids. You couldn't be a kid around him. He hated friends playing in the back yard. Anything out of his neat little order—forget it—it was no good.

"And all of that is inside of me! God! I've lived all my life by his rules. Without them I don't know who I am."

Deep understanding of the knowledge that he had incorporated his father and was living by those rules and not his own helped to free John from his inner tyranny. In addition, his new-found ability to be angry helped resolve his dependency on his father. And because John no longer felt forced to attack himself on every pretext, his moods became more stable.

In one of his dreams, called "The Lion Is a Pussycat," John is stalked by a dangerous lion who he fears will maim him or eat him up. In real life his analyst, whom he has seen as his protector, is going on vacation. In the dream she walks away and leaves him at the mercy of the lion. He feels frightened and unprotected.

"I am in a small car. A woman is driving. Then it stopped. There is a wild mountain lion, with fur around its head, coming up to the other side of the car. I am scared; I knew he wanted to get in the car, on the passenger side. I blocked it. So he goes around to the driver's side of the car. A woman opens the door (Is it you?) and walks away (You are going on vacation) and leaves me alone in the car. The lion jumps on me. I'm terrified. But then I see it's tame—it's not a lion at all—it's more like a pussycat.

"Last weekend when I went home, Saturday morning at eight o'clock, Dad called, 'Time to get up!' I thought, 'Why is it time to get up at eight o'clock on Saturday morning?' So I went back to bed. Then their cat jumped on my bed and scared me. So I sent it out of the room. 'Yeah,' I thought, 'why is it time to get up?' So I lazed in bed."

"And did Dad say anything?" the analyst asked.

"No," John answered.

"So he really is a pussycat," the analyst responded softly.

"Yes," John said. "In the dream there were lots of wild animals all around, but they really were all tame." Then in the turning point of the analysis, he added, "I guess it's only the father in my head I'm afraid of, and not my real father at all."

When the patient understands that the danger he has run from exists only in his head and not in reality, he no longer is at the mercy of his pathological fear and is well on the way to recovery. This dream, which indicated that John had met perhaps the most important criterion for a successful analysis, heralded the beginning of the termination phase of his analysis.

Optimal functioning requires a balance between inhibition and giving oneself permission to obtain and enjoy pleasure. John's difficulty along these lines lay in an excessive perception of danger, which caused him to grossly inhibit both his functioning and ability to experience pleasure. As he worked through his fear of his father, he had a dream in which he permitted himself to buy a good quality ice cream cone, in contrast to the cheap brand he usually bought at the supermarket. At this point his inhibitions began to seem excessive to him and even a bit silly. He began to allow pleasure to seep into his life, as he integrated the connection between his relationship with his strict father and his own inhibitions. A noteworthy breakthrough came when he impulsively allowed himself to tell the analyst that he loved his girlfriend's breasts.

Early in his treatment, John developed a strong positive relationship with me. This enabled him to work through a sustained period of mourning for his mother, which proved a further mile-stone in his treatment. His inhibitions had prevented him from grieving for her because he could not bear to experience the profound sorrow that would have followed. This changed in a relatively short time.

"Last night," he said, "I was listening to records about love, and I thought of you and how important you are to me. And I just started to bawl. I thought of Mom dying, and other people that are gone."

Then he began to "bawl" for his mother, too. As he learned to grieve, his depression lifted and gradually disappeared. This newfound ability to mourn turned out to be an important component in the lifting of his depression and provided him with the energy he needed to conduct his life.

John also relived many of his adolescent conflicts in his analysis. For example:

"When I was a kid," he said, "I had to go to the supermarket with Mom. I was bored. She dragged me over there every Saturday—I hated it. I wanted to be home doing something else. I remember going into a local store with Dad and seeing all the other kids in there. I wished I were there without Dad.

"As a teenager, we had Sunday dinners with Grandmother. I was furious that I had to spend Sundays that way. I was tied up with a belt. The belt that tied me up was that I was unable to say, 'I want to be with my friends.' I couldn't be angry.

"I'm thinking if I were a kid again, I'd go out with the guys more. I'd stay out late, past the time I had to be in."

"You were too afraid of your father," the analyst said.

"Yes," John replied. "He was a big man. Mom was afraid of him, too. No one stood up to him. . . . He was just a man. If I had stood up to him, he would have stopped the teasing. And he would have been closer to me."

John relived his unsatisfactory adolescence and brought it to an adequate conclusion. This enabled him to begin to stand up to his father and other authorities in his life.

John had another problem with his mother; he saw her as trying to seduce him. This is clearly expressed in a dream about his relationship with Jane, with whom he formed a sexual relationship midway through his analysis. The dream is as follows:

"An image of a very ugly woman—a witch—is coming at me. Who is this? I saw a movie with Jane called *Passion d'Amour*. A terribly ugly, sick woman demanded of this handsome guy that he make love to her. She pulled him into her web. She pulls him down, and at the end he gets her illness. This is Jane, her helplessness, her dependency; she'll trap me and pull me down with her. She has to be stopped, punished."

Jane is Oriental, very different from him and his family, and in many ways an unsuitable life partner. They have a very intense, sadomasochistic relationship. They torment each other and usually follow up the torture with sex of exquisite intensity. John is obsessed with her and picks at her constantly, as his father did at him. In associations to the dream, he says:

"I picture Jane bending over the high part of a chair. I slap her as she holds on to the chair. With each slap she holds on tighter. With each slap there is a jerking motion. In the movie [*Passion d'Amour*] there is pain in the guy's face. He is condemned to forty lashes. After a while you don't feel pain. That's what happened to me. It's been going on so long between my father and me that I don't feel any more pain.

"After it was over, after he hit me, he would kiss me. That's what I do to Jane."

The analyst says, "She is the sexual you, the bad you who has to be punished and then loved. So you beat her up for being like the part of you that Dad squelched, and then you forgive her with a kiss."

John agrees. He now understands that Jane is not his mother and that erotic feelings for his girlfriend are desirable and undeserving of punishment. As a result he finds himself able to sustain a satisfactory sexual relationship.

John experienced another difficulty in his relationship with Jane. He had never been as close to anyone as he was to her, and it terrified him enough to have the following nightmare:

"Someone had squeezed through the gate of my window. The apartment was all torn apart. There was black dust inside and out. I went for the bathrobe where I keep my money for the week. The laundry bag was dumped, and a blue shirt that I like was lying on top of the heap of laundry. I woke up, feeling that I wasn't robbed.

"The someone is Jane. She has squeezed through a spot into me. I am very scared that she will rob me of myself, but I don't have to worry about that. She'll just make a mess of my internal life—upset my balance. Somehow she has crept through, crept through someplace that was left unguarded. . . . My heart is beating very fast. But in the dream, she doesn't rob me, just shakes everything up. She shakes up my identity—my core—who I am."

According to W. Meissner, the sense of self is organized around such internal images as John maintained of his father.[2] Meissner states that "however desperate, conflicted, vulnerable, dependent, victimized, entitled, or omnipotent that pathological self may be. . . . such a sense of self is, after all, the best that the patient has been able to do through the vicissitudes of a lifetime." Loss of a sense of self brings terror in its wake. In John's dream, the image of his father has disappeared. As a result, his apartment is all torn up. Jane's creeping inside of him has "shaken up his core." Instead of resorting to his former neurotic behavior, however, he tolerates his terror without defenses or regression.

John's sense of self has been strengthened and is preparing him for an intimate relationship with less fear of loss of identity. His self-enhancement becomes evident in a later dream in which he was riding to work on the subway. Overhead was a little niche from which a strap hung. John held on to the strap. "I guess I've found my niche in life," he said.

John recovered many childhood memories in his analysis, including the most painful of all, that of his parents having sexual intercourse. The distress of his analyst's impending vacation awakened repressed memories in John of how he had felt as a child on hearing his parents make love. The memories returned via this dream:

"I am at the bottom of the steps of a long stairway," he dreamed. "I'm trapped at the bottom of the stairs. There is a metal fence with barbed wire at the top. I'm huddled in the corner trying to cover myself up. Like a prisoner of war. Someone at the top threw me down there—a woman, you! You threw me down there! You are going on vacation. You are throwing me out!

"The staircase—it is the staircase at home: My brother and I spent a lot of time playing there. I'm trapped down there— Mom and Dad's bedroom is overhead. I had to listen. We could hear them having sex."

A few weeks before, John had "forgotten" that he had shown me a picture of his parents dancing. My questioning of his lapse of memory was able to elicit from him a memory of the first time he found out about intercourse as a young teenager. His response at the time was, "Not my parents!" This led to further recollections of his parents' closed door every Saturday morning and the misery John experienced waiting for his mother to come and make his breakfast. The episode is reminiscent of a statement by renowned psychoanalyst Jacob Arlow: "The primal scene [of parental intercourse] is never quite remembered and never quite forgot."[3]

Analysis of this dream equipped John to live with the knowledge that his parents were lovers, without a great deal of anxiety. It also helped him to accept his mother's seductiveness in an undisguised form and to allow himself to be like his sexual father. Shortly thereafter, he dreamed:

"A mother and a little boy. Yesterday I saw a middle-aged Spanish woman with her little boy at her side. She reaches down to straighten her nylons. I'm surprised. She raises her skirt, is real seductive. I said, 'What's going on here?' It could be me and Mom. She did that all the time, lifted her skirt and fixed her nylons. My eyes followed the woman.

"I'm leaning against the door—just like Dad. He's a big, strong man with huge arms. I scratch my back on the doorway like he does."

In permitting himself to be attracted to his mother and sexual like his father, without too much fear of retribution, John has taken a giant step forward in the resolution of his Oedipus complex. Whereas he once bolted in horror at the idea of wanting to make love to his mother, he has learned to accept the normal development that every little boy passes through. This became the basis of a new sexuality with the woman he loved.

When all goes well in the development of children, they have an inner image of a good mother that sustains them in her absence. John had never been able to internalize his good mother. As a result, when she died he lost her presence in an emotional sense as well as the physical. One day late in his treatment he dreamed that he was walking on the beach and looking up at the moon. As he walked, the moon moved with him. "Wherever I went, the moon went, too," he said. He associated that with summers he had walked on the beach with his mother.

Then he added, "You are my moon. Wherever I go, you will go with me."

This last statement informs us that John no longer needed the physical presence of his analyst for him to feel that she was with him. Thus he could afford to leave her.

There were many other indications that John was preparing to terminate analysis. For example, he had worshiped and idealized his mother all his life. Gradually but consistently over the course of the analysis, the image of her as omnipotent, omniscient, and constantly available faded away. He became able to tolerate negative as well as positive feelings toward her.

In similar fashion, he had overidealized me, thought my achievements were far beyond his reach, pictured me as very rich and living in a mansion. When the patient overidealizes the analyst, it is at the expense of his image of himself. As John gradually scaled down the image of his parents, he was able to enlarge his view of his own person and powers.

For John, discriminating between the image of his father of childhood and the analyst in the present meant that he himself was competent and potent. Thus, it was crucial that he become able to distinguish aggression from masculinity and see himself as masculine in what he could achieve rather than purely in the macho image of his father. Differentiating himself from the powerful likeness of his father helped John to oppose those rules and traits that he did not want to carry with him into adult life. It enabled him to become his own man. He has opted for fewer rules, less harsh enforcement of the dictates he will live by, and stronger links between his rules and their consequences.

His image of himself became more realistic as the analysis proceeded. He perceived himself as more powerful, autonomous, and valuable. He saw both his parents as having worthwhile as well as unfortunate qualities. Representations of his parents in his girlfriend and in the analyst became superfluous as he grew to understand his life in terms of his earlier relationships. He was then free to terminate with both Jane and the analyst because he no longer needed them as actors in his internal drama.

The leveling out of the disparate images of himself and his analyst became clear the day he met me walking my dog.

John observed with surprise, "That dog is just an ordinary mutt, not a pedigreed dog at all! You are just a human being like me. If you can go to school and get as far as you have, then I can do it, too." The analyst agreed.

John had obsessed about Jane for eight long years. Although they tried several times, he never succeeded in separating from her without going into a deep depression. When he realized that I was "just a human being" like him, he was able to relinquish the idea that someday he would possess the woman of his dreams. Then he could leave his girlfriend and meet a more suitable life companion, whom he eventually married.

In addition, because he was able to allow his analyst to be an ordinary human being with ordinary human limitations, he could accept that he, too, was a person with flaws. He no longer needed to demand perfection of himself or of others.

About the same time, John began to experience a different kind of support from his father than he ever had before. When he felt the need to increase the number of analytic sessions, his father paid for the increase in cost. John began to see his father as he saw the analyst, as encouraging his masculine strivings, in contrast to his mother who had babied him. As a child he had adored his mother and feared and hated his father. Now, negative feelings for his mother developed along with positive feelings for his father. Thus John became more realistic about both his parents and their relationship with him. He also found that he could tolerate negative feelings about his father, when they were experienced in the context of his anger at the analyst for going on vacation.

"How dare you leave me in the middle of all this?" John had raged. "I'm raw with this superego thing and my dilemma with Jane. And, anyway, who ever heard of an analyst going away for two weeks in April? It's not like you. And who needs you anyway? I don't need you!"

This tirade was followed by a further outburst of fury against his father. Feeling outrage at the analyst and then his father enabled John to recognize that previous prohibitions against expressing anger were coming from himself, not the outside world. His view of his father changed dramatically when he realized that the older man was not terrifying, not threatening, and not even up to John's own standards. Seeing these people as so very ordinary gave John the opportunity to form an altered view of his own size and potency. When he visualized his formerly unconscious image of himself as small and puny in contrast to his father, he was able to see that actually they were very much the same size.

"I had a thought about my career and my father's today," John said. "I'm way ahead of him. I thought, 'You know what? I'm much smarter than he is. He's nowhere near as smart as I am. I don't have to be afraid of him anymore.'"

In addition to changing his actual relationship with his father, this discovery freed him to be appropriately angry when attacked and to stand up for his rights with people he loved.

His insight also helped him become skilled at dealing with other conflict-laden material. In place of the shame he once felt about his homosexual feelings for his macho father, John found himself dealing openly with them. This led him to realize that he really did not want to be a homosexual but wished to have a wife and a family.

In addition, the relief he experienced in his diminution of symptoms led to many changes in his daily functioning. Whereas John's counselor had sent him for treatment because his unhappiness was interfering with his studying, he now was able to concentrate and make progress in his chosen profession. Evenings spent at home crying alone had long been a thing of the past.

In his associations to the "Oedipal dream," John found himself mourning his father's aging and loss of power as well as inevitable death, thus fulfilling the dreaded desire of the Oedipal boy to replace his father. After facing the little boy's wish to possess his mother, John had interrupted his associations by hitting himself on the head. Then he began to attack himself as he used to.

"What's the matter with me always having to be like him? Why can't I be central?" he complained.

"Why did you run away?" the analyst asked. "You had an image of yourself as a big strong man like your father. And then you had to bring yourself down, to hit and belittle yourself. What did you feel before you began the attack?"

John responded in tears. "I felt very sad. He's not big and strong anymore, the way he used to be. He's old and weary. Instead of working hard all day long, now he can only do a little bit each day. If I hit myself, I can stay a little boy. And I can keep him young and strong."

This new awareness removed what was probably the last impediment to John's acceptance of himself as a man, lover, husband, and father.

In one of the final dreams in the series, John pictures himself driving his father's pickup truck home. Along the way he finds that there are many hazards to avoid. For example, a large steel rod looms at him from the left, and on the right is a narrow track in which he fears the truck will get stuck. Among other interpretations, I understood these dangers to represent his fear of moving ahead at the same time that he was anxious of remaining stuck. John picks up the truck "like a superman" and lifts it up over the obstacles. Whatever the danger, "he keeps on steering the truck."

John's awareness of his own strength, formerly a source of terror to him, now has become a comfort. The dream image of lifting a truck with superhuman strength dramatically represents this awareness. In that dream, he first expresses fury at his overly strict and joyless father and then is able to voice his rage at the rules he carries inside himself. His range of emotions has broadened considerably, as he manages to express defiance of his father, ambivalence toward him, and pleasure in his "bad" feelings.

This dream predicts that whatever impediments John may meet in his analysis and in his life, he will always try to "keep on steering the truck." For however skilled and talented an analyst may be, the crucial element in the success or failure of every analysis lies in the degree of courage possessed by the patient. It takes valor and fortitude to face what one has dreaded knowing all one's life. Without a sufficient amount of those qualities, no analysis can be successful. Here, indeed, character is destiny. The dream confirms that John is a very courageous man. The prognosis for his analysis and his life is very good indeed.

Showing remarkable progress from his early insightless days, John became a master at the interpretation of his own dreams. Once when the analyst commended him for his excellent work with them, he responded:

"Dreams are my only hope—the way to get in touch. During the day my superego rules me. Every night I come into my own. When I don't dream, I take it as a sign that something is wrong— that I really am cut off from myself." This ability to analyze his own dreams is an important signal he is nearing the end of his analysis and is ready to take over the analyst's role.

Affirming his insight of the importance of dreams, John's first intimations that he was getting ready to terminate his analysis also came from a dream. He said to the analyst:

"You were making plans for a summer vacation. You were giving me the name of a therapist in case I needed help. The name of the therapist was Noonan Summer. I thought, 'She never did this before. Why now?'

"The name Summer stands for your summer vacation. Noon is 12 o'clock. I said good-bye to an intake worker at noon yesterday. We threw a party. She said a formal good-bye. I didn't think it was final, but she did."

The analyst was silent for a few minutes. "You are saying good-bye to me," she said sadly. "You are preparing to leave the analysis."

Perhaps most important of all for John's future as an independent, self-sufficient person is this ability to take over the analyst's role. In an important sense he has become his own analyst and no longer is dependent on me. This was borne out after his termination, when he lived through some very difficult times, including the death of his brother. But because of the analyst within him, he has never found it necessary to return for further treatment.

In his final dream of the analysis, John is speaking to the analyst on a cordless phone. "I guess I've cut the cord to you," he said. In the dream he has moved into a beautiful new house with his new wife. "I like it much better than the old house," he says, "even though it cost a lot of money." The new house stands for himself as he is now. He likes this new self much more than the old one, although indeed the change has been expensive, both emotionally and financially. The dream predicts the resolution of his dependency on the analyst, his ability to achieve a satisfactory marriage, and the success of his life after the termination of analysis.

And in reality the dream predictions are borne out. For John is now a happily married professional who is extremely successful in his work and, indeed, in his life.

Life Begins after Analysis:
A Case History

Sally Summers is a woman whose life did not truly begin until after her analysis was over. Depressed and dependent, she spent most of her time trying to force love from reluctant partners and was often preoccupied with suicidal thoughts. Not much time or energy was left over for Sally to live a life.

She came into analysis with me when she was twenty-three years old. She was referred by a colleague who diagnosed Sally as schizophrenic, and who was seeing her in group therapy. He felt she required more intensive treatment than she could get in a group. She was in analysis with me for many years, often coming for as many as five sessions a week. She was very fragile, and for much of the treatment found it necessary to supplement her sessions with numerous letters and phone calls. Despite her illness, however, she experienced as close to a complete cure as I have ever seen in any patient.

She was a pretty, slender young woman with a lively intensity and an ability to throw herself into whatever interested her that should have alerted me to the likelihood of her potential "cure,"—despite the degree of her illness.

And she was very ill indeed! Her dependency on me for regaining her strength and health was almost complete. I knew that one false move could have meant her life. She made several suicide attempts during the analysis. Before one of them, I received the following letter:

> I am sober, so that you know my wish to die is not a chemically induced one. I have convinced myself that I don't like this world, this planet—and what man and mankind have grown into. I decided I am right about life's not being such a great favor. And I really don't care about how everybody must make compromises; how not everybody can have his or her way all the time. Everybody else is hooked on this life—the life of the homo sapiens. I'm simply not.
>
> There will be no dramatics in this suicide. I happen not to feel the least bit dramatic. Just bored. Some of my friends will be hurt that I did not write them a final letter. So do me a favor, Alma. Tell them for me that I simply do not have the impetus, the instinct, or whatever to ease their pain. Tell them I've no respect for them anyway anymore. They all try so hard to "make it" in this life, and I've grown way beyond that.
>
> It's too late. Too late. I'm all washed out. I was born deformed and thus I can't "make it." You and my friends can call upon Freud and rationalize what I mean by "deformed."
>
> As for my possessions, I don't really care what happens to them. I do care about my books. Why don't you save them for your children? What you don't want, bury with me. That's all I care about. Tiredness is not merely being weary. It's being realistic. I don't like this world of mine, world of ours. Perhaps if I were ten years younger. But I'm not, and I choose not to spend the rest of my days wishing I were ten years younger. So, I have inherited something from my father after all. The desire to die—the strongest, or at least the most real desire I've ever had.
>
> How will I kill myself? A gun is the most appealing. But if it's too complicated to get one, then I shall try pills and alcohol.

When? I don't know. All I need is to feel a little more tired. Just a little more. If you miss me and it's painful, I'm sorry. But it's not my fault that you, like the others, could not face reality.

Although she did not kill herself, Sally suffered at least one psychotic breakdown requiring hospitalization during the course of her analysis. When I went to the hospital to continue her treatment, I was told by the attending psychiatrist to "forget all about her. She is schizophrenic and will never get well."

A symptom of the seriousness of her sometimes total inability to tolerate frustration was clearly demonstrated when she bought an expensive new electric typewriter, which she was unable to get to function. In order to avoid the frustration involved, she completely destroyed the machine.

One night I gave her a session at 2 A.M. because I felt her life depended on it. I'll never forget her response. She said, "Big deal! You think it's so wonderful of you to see me at 2 A.M. You don't realize that's just a drop in the bucket compared to what I need!"

She was so debilitated by my absence one summer that I allowed her to come to a town where I was vacationing, and we held a marathon session for eight hours that seemed to sustain her until the summer ended.

During the marathon, Sally had a very significant experience. It occurred when this buried memory came to the surface.

She said, "It was sunny outside. I was crawling around on the floor. I was wearing only a diaper and a shirt. I can remember the rough feel of the rug against my body. When they went out, I could see the sunlight under the crack in the door. I lay there on the floor watching that crack and waiting, waiting, waiting. I cried. I screamed. For a long, long time. Then I stopped.

"I was hungry. I was so hungry it hurt. But I didn't know how to go get a bottle, so I just lay there hurting and staring at the light under the door.

"After a while the light under the door grew dimmer and then dark. Still I watched. Still no one came. I stopped crying.

"I think I gave up then. Something in me died that day. I must have been around six months old. I know it. But that was the day I died. Oh, they came back all right. But it was too late. The damage was already done.

"They came back—happy. She was laughing gaily. She picked me up, still laughing, as though nothing at all had happened. She put me in my crib with a bottle. Can you imagine? After all that time, she put me in my crib with a bottle and went away. I was stunned. The bottle fell out of my mouth, but I couldn't pick it up. So it lay there all night long.

"Now can you see why I hate the sunlight?

"I can't let *you* go, because how would I know if I'll ever see you again?"

The force of this buried memory, and I believe it is a screen memory representing many similar incidents, was the trigger for Sally's pathological yearnings as an adult. Her most painful symptom was her terrible dependency on the person with whom she was involved, in this case me, so that she was in agony if the loved one was out of sight. For many years she felt she could not survive the time between her sessions without writing me a letter or phoning. A weekend away was an eternity for Sally, and a month was a vast wasteland she felt she could not survive. This terror resulted in a hold that often felt stultifying to the object of her affections. Despite Sally's loving, generous nature, cooperative spirit, intelligence, and delightful sense of humor, her desperate neediness always alienated her lovers.

Sally seemed to get sicker and sicker. A few weeks later, I was horrified to receive the following letter:

Dear Alma:

People do not kill themselves because of a love affair gone wrong. They kill themselves because an early tenderness went wrong. I believe that babies and young children who do not have anxiety-free caressing from parents or parent figures are doomed to die. The lucky ones die early. The unlucky ones, myself, wait until old age gets them. And no amount of verbalizing can move them. They, like me, flounder from one affair to the next. Caressing becomes an all-consuming obsession. And really, where can obsessions lead except to stronger ones? Each obsession serves as fuel for the next. And how do obsessions start? Well, we all are born with a healthy-sized potential for obsession and all we need to trigger it off is pseudotenderness, or anxious caressing and—boom—there it is!

Well, I'm going to try to fool my personality. I'm gonna try not to live until old age with it.

Die. I want to die. Somebody. Anybody. Alma? Hey Mother, how about you? You've always wanted to kill me, anyway. How about doing it now? *Now* Now Now.

S.

Around this time, I sent Sally for psychological testing. The report of the psychologist stated:

The Rorschach record varies considerably in quality. It suggests that the patient is able to select from a situation the most obvious and ordinary details and react to them; however, her elaborations upon those details and her reactions to emotionally loaded situations are distorted by strong projections and primitive needs. She seems to use reality as a point of departure for fantasies and seems unable to analyze critically the appropriateness of her impressions.

The tendency to establish idiosyncratic relationships between details, and to stress the meaning of rather irrelevant components suggest that the patient is undergoing a schizoid process with paranoid thinking. Some of the content involving mutilation and deformity also suggests depressive features. Reality appears to her extremely threatening, and the picture she has

of herself is that of an undifferentiated, embryonic being, threatened by disintegration.

That Sally herself was devastated by her state of mind is
apparent in the following letter:

Dear Mind:

You've really flipped, haven't you? You don't listen to the news
anymore. You don't listen to music unless you're high. You don't
buy the *Times*. You don't make your bed. You keep the shades at
home drawn. You don't clean your house. Everything is just lying
around. You wash yourself but with tremendous effort, and you
do so with anger, belligerence. But at least you do it. That's something. You don't read books anymore. You want to read but won't.
Your *Science Digest* magazine tempts you, but you deny it. You're
a mess.

You drink a helluva lot. You mention a nice, pleasant high.
You don't know how to socialize anymore without it. You can't
even stay on your job without drinking. And so brazen. You put
ice cubes in your coffee cup and pour in the vodka and sit it on
your desk. It does not smell, which is why you've chosen vodka.
And it looks like water. You're clever, but are really acting dumb
now. Your wit is dulled. Your humor is nil. You are a mess.

Dear, dear mind. What has happened to you? Why are you
such a slob now? Why are your desert boots your most important possession? Why are they the only things for which you feel
affection? Real affection? Why do you cherish them?

Mind, why do you keep twisting and turning onto the dark,
scary side of the road? Why is sunshine, in which I know you love
to bathe, such an enemy? Why is even the milky grey light of a
cloudy day so offensive to your eyes? And your eyes—why, mind,
are they so tense, so unseeing, so tragic, so deathly frightened?

Dear, dear mind. What is your answer? Why are you letting
yourself decay? Don't you want to live? Don't you want to be part

of this earth? Don't you want to care, to feel, to love again, to be loved? I cry for you. Please try to answer me.

Your owner,

S.

Shortly thereafter, in what appeared a sudden, unprecipitated move, Sally left New York for several weeks to roam the country, in a psychotic state, without informing me or anyone else of her whereabouts. Needless to say, friends, family, and I were all in a panic about her welfare. But something healthy was growing in Sally, in the soil of her psychosis. She was gaining insight into the basic cause of her illness. At the end of her wanderings, I received the following poignant and insightful letter:

Dear Alma:

I see that it is 8 P.M. I am amazed at how the time dissolves here. You see—not having to wait to see you, to be with you, not having to go through the agony of fifty minutes a day, makes the time pass. But God almighty—I need you every day. And if it can only be fifty minutes, then O.K. I will go through the countdown, the blastoff, the blinding rocket fire, the quick descent into cold, anonymous outer space every goddam day—until I can leave by the front door rather than by a missile pad.

Yes. Yes. Each time I leave you, it is [like] being ejected from my mother's womb. Yes. . . . And oh, God, how I want to be back there! I sincerely believe that I *do* remember my whole birth experience. I think it came back to me when I saw myself as a crawling baby on the carpet in the room that was growing dark. And the memory never let go. It adhered to me like a blood-sucking leech.

All things told, Alma, I'm not doing badly. I am now tumbling, catapulting, head over heels through that twilight zone—the descent from the womb to the world.

A long, long journey. There are many horrors on the way, many changes in direction—up, down, up, down, sideways, falling smoothly, falling jerkily—with the birth membrane smothering me all the way—with the streaks of my mother's blood coursing down my body. With the remnants of afterbirth in my eyes, my mouth, my nose. A tiny infant, newborn. But already filled with an intensity of sensations that not even an adult should feel.

I need you, Alma. I feel I must recreate in a wide span of time this falling. You see—once my mother let go of me from her womb, I never really saw, felt, smelled her again. Not really. A child was born without a mother. And I want to be born again *with* a mother. Oh, please hear me. When once again I am ejected from that orange balloon (which is what the womb must have looked like to me), I want you to be there. How else can I dare to let myself be born again? Once without a mother was enough.

Love,

Sally

For several years after this episode, all was quiet with Sally, as she worked through her insights in the analysis. She gradually returned to her usual sunny disposition, and her customary life of work, hobbies, and friends. It was a period of relative peace and tranquillity, as her yearnings became more subdued, and she learned to sublimate them in poetry. She read a great deal of it, and published many of her own poems in the "little" magazines.

But she was not yet ready to let go of her illness completely, of course. For just as I began to believe we were "over the hill" and that she was truly well, the following shocker arrived in the mail:

Dear Alma:

There is no more hope for me in seeing you. You have taken me very, very far and I will be deeply thankful for that as long as

I live. It's so strange . . . people with my problems and needs can really turn to no one but an analyst for help. And yet seeing you is still a torment to me, and I do not have whatever it takes to live with and accept the torment. So long as I see you, I will never cease wanting to be yours—I will never cease wanting you to feel ecstasy and love from loving me. I cannot be analyzed, Alma, not by you or anyone else ever again.

I realize this means I will be searching the rest of my life. And I will keep finding temporary sustenance. But at least the breast will be real. I know you think I only feel this way *now* and that someday I will find someone else to love. I think I have tried. I found it for a while with a man, but that was impossible, too, right from the start.

All this time with you I never let go of the hope that you would want me as I want you to want me. And finally, I see and know it is a fruitless hope.

All my love,

S.

P.S. Oh, God, I wish I had the strength to tear this page up. But I don't. Catch me, Alma. I don't want to be saved from this emotional suicide, and yet I feel compelled to beg you to catch me—to try to help me learn to sit up again.

I will not save myself. That is not a weakness, it is not a threat. It is my sickness, my running away from you and whatever you are. I will run but will be praying that you will call me back to you.

Alma, you are the mightiest nightmare I have ever had. Bring me back to the terror again. Please.

Love,

S.

Before I had time to integrate the letter and decide what to do about it, another arrived on its tail. Sally had spent so much money roaming the countryside and had needed so many extra sessions that she was now heavily in debt. She wrote:

> Dear Alma:
>
> I would like to try again, even though I don't know whether that's healthy or masochistic at this point. First I have to give you the financial details, and you will have to decide whether or not you can continue seeing me.
>
> [The next part of the letter deals with her financial situation, and how she expected to repay me for the sessions.]
>
> The decision is yours. If you decide you cannot see me because of all this, I don't know how I'll feel. The only thing I can offer you now is myself and every honest effort to work with you rather than against you. I know that being an analyst is your job—your means of earning a living, and I guess like everything else, if you can't afford to pay for a service, you simply can't have it.
>
> Love,
> S.

I allowed Sally to mount up an unbelievably large debt, the most money any patient ever owed me. She paid back every cent after she finished her analysis. Treating a patient "on the cuff" is not advised as good analytic procedure. The patient is considered to be "acting out," and generally is asked to leave and return when his or her financial situation improves. I felt I had no choice with Sally but to continue. We analyzed thoroughly what the "indulgence," as it is called in analysis, meant to her. I don't believe my trusting her impeded the analysis one bit. In fact I am most happy I did.

Sally recovered from this phase of her illness with the deep conviction that she had never had enough mothering and that the urgency with which she had sought it belonged to the time of her infancy, not now. This insight put to rest her obsession with being mothered and afforded her several years of emotional peace, as her need for me gradually subsided.

Her new lightness of heart about her analyst is evident in the following poem:

Get Well Soon
(An Analyst Speaks Her Mind)

Rock-a-bye patient
On your analyst's couch,
Speak of your daddy,
That rotten ol' grouch.
Speak of your mama,
Who wanted to be
Sister and father and lover
    to thee.

Rock-a-bye patient
In your analyst's room,
Let go your feelings,
Go back to the womb.
Let yourself feel well or neurotic,
Feel terribly sterile or wildly erotic.

Rock-a-bye patient
In this—your hour,
Feel terribly weak,
Or drunk with power.
Feel with your heart,
Or feel with your hands,
Your analyst certainly understands.

Rock-a-bye patient,
You're safe (if not sound)
Lie perfectly still,
Or dash all around.
Spill out your fears,
Your blood, sweat, and guts,
And be quick, dear patient,
. . . You're driving me nuts.

But the Sturm and Drang still was not over for Sally. We had gone through and survived the pain and suffering caused by her inadequate relationship with her mother and ended her desperate search for mothering. But in every analysis, a patient must relive his or her experiences with father as well as mother. One patient, on finding this out, said, "I went through all this with my mother. Do you mean I have to go through it all over again with my father?" The answer to that patient was yes.

Thus Sally entered the next, penultimate phase of her analysis, which concentrated on the death of her father, when she was eight years old. His loss had left her bereft and empty, and was a significant factor in her passionate attempts to return to the womb, as she sought to escape the memory of the pain of his death.

Perhaps the most important setback in her relationship with her father was triggered by a remark he made to her when he thought he was dying. This remark she experienced as more traumatic than his actual death. For whatever reason, he told Sally that although he loved her, he had always loved her brother, Bob, more. Sally was devastated and had never recovered from her father's remark. Nevertheless, she did not become psychotic at this difficult point in her analysis, or indeed, ever again. But the suffering he caused her is apparent in this letter she wrote to her dead father, as she approached the end of her analysis:

Dear Father:

For so long now, Father, I have out of fear and pain pretended that you never told me you loved Bobby more than me. It must have hurt you to say that; I cannot believe that it didn't. You had had a heart attack, you thought you were dying. It must have been that all along you felt guilty because you loved or thought you loved Bobby more than me. But, oh, Father, I never would have known. For if you did feel that way, you kept it well. I always felt you loved me very deeply, I always felt proud to be with you because *your* pride in *me* made me walk sprightly and tall.

I remember so well my new spring coat. Maybe I was eight or nine. It was a very-light-green tweed with a pink silky lining. I wore a brown felt bonnet with it, which had a long brown ribbon that blew in the wind. I remember walking with you in the park with that outfit, and you were beaming. You liked the way I looked.

I knew, too, that when you'd come home from work you would look for me as you came down the block, just as hard as I looked and waited for you. I'd run to you and hug and kiss you, and almost always you had candy for Bobby and me. It used to break my heart, Daddy, to see you walking so slowly, breathing so hard, or trying to catch your breath. But you were a proud man and you had to work, no matter how painful it was, no matter how sore your dear heart.

I knew, too, that you loved having me sit on your lap as much as I loved to. I used to play with your earlobes (I have not yet found earlobes as soft) and we would laugh.

There were times you scolded and hit me, but those times do not stand out in my mind, because the love you felt for me always came through. I don't remember ever feeling unloved by you; I don't ever remember feeling you loved Bobby more or me less. If that was so, I'm sorry you didn't take that feeling to the grave with you. For that confession has not served me well. Only now am I finding out that the day you said that is the day you really died for me, and something very vital, very alive, and very necessary died in me, too.

But I no longer will punish you and myself for it. And I will restore again your love, not your confession. And in so doing, I will restore my own love, too. My heart is still young and strong, and I know now that it cannot die, even when I try.

I came home to you that day to help you. Mom was working, Bob was, too. I had been playing. I came home to help you, to save you, so that you would not die. And in the end, we both did. Oh, Father, what made a kind man like you say such brutal words to a small child who loved you?

Well, I shall not keep seeking your image, to prove to myself that I cannot ever really be loved. No, I will not settle for that ever again. I loved you, I have missed you, I am glad I had that even for a short while. But I no longer want to join you in your grave. I know if you could hear me now there would be tears in your eyes and joy in your heart.

Sally's insights about her father freed her for the first time to try to develop a real relationship with a man. She looked for two years, but somehow never was able to find a satisfactory male partner. I discussed her case with a class I was teaching, and they felt that she had been freed to have the *option* of developing a heterosexual relationship, and this was all any analysis could do. Be that as it may, Sally lived very comfortably as a celibate until several years later, when she found her life partner. They are still living together in a relationship that seems to deepen and grow richer with the passing years.

When I signed a contract to write this book, I thought of Sally. She had written me literally hundreds of letters during her time of need, and I thought perhaps she would enjoy writing one of vastly different content.

I was delighted to receive the following letter from her a week or so after I contacted her:

Dear Alma:

Well, here it is—in all its "whatever-came-to-mind-barely edited" glory. I'm sure it's no accident the Before Analysis section is the shortest—perhaps because *life really did begin after analysis* (to answer the question in your book title).

I took myself by surprise when the prose suddenly began to flow into poetry, as you will see by the last three pages.

In writing the prose, my tendency was either to be very brief ("From Mess to Mensch") or to pour and pour and pour—and so I, absolutely spontaneously, flowed into poetry, which succinctly balances the extremes.

This was quite an experience, putting me forcefully in touch with what was and what is. God, how strong we were to have survived me!

Do use my name.[1] I am who I am, and I went through hell to find that "am," and darned if I want to hide me now. Whatever reactions there might be, no matter from whom, negative or positive, I know I'll be able to deal with them.

Understatement of the year: I look forward to the book.

Love,

Sally

Sally describes her life before and after analysis.

Before Analysis

Life was a desperate search for instant gratification, for approval, for being loved constantly. I smothered those I loved and needed to be smothered in return. I fled from feelings of anger—they were squelched for so long that they became overwhelming monsters, their origins lost somewhere in inner space. I fled from mourning childhood losses, particularly the death of my father when I was eight, lest the memories of and grief for those I lost drown me. My relationships with lovers were consumed with anxiety—to love was to lose. Time spent without them was time spent thinking of nothing but being with them again. I was self-destructive in my quest for attention, in my denial of anger, in my wish to be safe with my dead father.

After Analysis

The fragments of my life, my self, were excavated, scraped, dusted off. From beneath the layers, my identity emerged. Now anxieties are easily understood and thus no longer last very long. Nor are they at all frequent. I feel so fortunate in being able to quickly separate what is from what was, to recognize the occasional reemergence of past ghosts, and to even smile at the recognition. Now I am a well-analyzed ghost buster.

In my relationship with Larry for thirteen years, I have grown and grown, for it is a rich and enriching connection. Larry is also very healthy, stable, intelligent, resourceful—and a helluva lot of fun. His involvement with and love for others makes me happy. There is not a shred of doubt in my mind or heart that what he feels for me is special, unique. I no longer need to be loved exclusively, nor do *I* have to love one person only—one *special* person, yes—but not *only*.

One of the most wonderful outcomes of my analysis is that I now have the luxury of loving to be with him, but also wanting, needing, and enjoying our times apart. To be able to be with others totally, without him, without obsessing and being anxious about being with him again is, for me, the height of emotional wealth. We both have the emotional capacity to let each other go, making our togetherness a delight of freedom.

Our arguments (sometimes fierce, but rare) always turn into learning more about ourselves and each other. We argue as passionately as we love—thus we argue well. Often we trigger each other's old ghosts, those annoying creatures who drop in unannounced, trying once again to get a free meal. But they don't stand a chance and are soon sent packing without much more than a crumb.

I am easily able to ask for what I want, need, and feel I deserve. (That came in very handy when I asked for and received a $5,000 salary adjustment!) And I now can wait calmly, if wait I must.

Larry and I are equally matched in the pleasure of giving to and taking from one another on all levels. And this, too, makes for much fullness.

Sometimes we both feel the fear of losing each other—with the aging process comes awareness of mortality, heightened by living in a crime-drenched city and the loss of friends, acquaintances, and coworkers to cancer and AIDS. But again, we are able to express these fears, talk about them to each other, and then happily return to the here and now, to the richness of our life together, and to the awareness of the abundance and wonders of life as a whole.

When my mother became seriously ill, and again when she died, I called Alma, my ex-analyst, even though it had been many years since the termination. It was a totally automatic reflex. And when Larry entered my life, I contacted Alma again, to share that joy with her. She was always there for me during analysis, and she is always there for me still. But I don't feel I need anything from her now, except to hear what I know are feelings of pure caring for me in times of stress, and true delight in my times of joy. Though I get that from others now, at particularly significant junctures in my life the picture is incomplete unless I bring Alma into it with me. And I like that.

Speaking of my mother's death—the first significant death in my life for many years—I was fine. That is, I wept, I mourned, I longed for her, I dreamt wonderfully clear dreams about her, I was not afraid of "that ol' floating feeling," that sensation of detachment from all things familiar—I knew that to feel these things was good, necessary—for not to feel them is to keep on floating.

> Before Analysis
>
> Buried alive,
> trying to break free,
> digging myself deeper,
> using thin shards,
> but needed a derrick.
> Now and then
> a breakthrough.
> Terrified by the light.
> Retreat, break down.
> Away from hope,

hope is death,
life the enemy.
Get close to death,
close to Father.
Safe.

During Analysis

Buried alive.
Someone offers a derrick,
makes me dig, uncover.
Avalanches. Terrors.
Breakdowns. Breakthroughs
to ancient caves.
Treasures emerge,
ladders of light.
Batwings release me,
damaged but alive.
Avalanches cease.
I weep in my
rescuer's hands,
leave the cave.

After Analysis

Rescuer no longer
nearby, but
always within.
I am content, strong.
Cave-ins happen still,
but
I am skilled
in working
the derrick.
Now I love
the night.
Now
I see the stars.

Part 3

Life after Analysis

7

What Takes the Place of Analysis?

As previously indicated, when all goes well in an analysis, the internalized figure of the analyst takes the place of his or her actual presence. In a manner of speaking, the primary motive of psychoanalysis is to make the analyst obsolete. In the beginning phases of analysis, we are the most important person in the world to our patients. But as the analysis proceeds, the patient gradually takes over the process itself, as well as the image of the analyst. Then, like beloved aging parents, we are no longer primary in the lives of our patients.

The image of the good-enough analyst must be incorporated as a part of the personality of the patient before the full benefit from analysis can be reaped. It is said that we are never really able to grow up until the death of our parents. So long as they live, we are still psychologically their child. I think the same can be said of patient and analyst. The patient must really let go of the actual analyst before the internalization process is complete.

The postanalytic phase is an extremely important time in the ex-patient's life. The analytic work continues in the form of further resolution and integration after the formal termination of the analysis. During this period, the analyst represents a symbol of access to the unconscious mind. To this degree, every analyst is a teacher. To put it differently, every analysis is a training analysis, which teaches the patient to analyze, to listen to the unconscious, and to observe the contents of his mind in a nonjudgmental manner.

This process is beautifully illustrated in a letter I received six months after the termination of her analysis from Bonnie, a tall, lovely twenty-six-year-old who had finished law school in the course of her analysis. Certain significant problems remained, and I would have liked her to continue in treatment for another year or so. But she felt she needed to leave, so I reluctantly agreed. Nevertheless, the letter demonstrates the success of her internalization of the analyst and the analyst's role. The internalization is still incomplete, but she continues to work with it toward the resolution of the Oedipus complex.

> Dear Alma:
>
> I recently saw a card that said, "It wouldn't be so hard to give you up if only you were here to help me with it." Thinking of you I sighed, because it was true. I miss you terribly. But I'm writing because there's another side to the truth.
>
> It wasn't until a few months ago that I realized I missed you so badly. The ongoing conversations I had with you didn't help much, not even the arguments I continued with you. But you were a constant presence.
>
> In the last two months I've had a number of dreams about you. In one, we have a pleasant erotic encounter. Then you leave for another room and close the door to me. Though I succeed in getting the door open, you scream at me and slap my face. I'm frightened and confused, perceiving you are upset because you've crossed a forbidden boundary. You again close the door to me and I'm afraid you are going to kill yourself.

Though my death wishes against you are apparent, what felt more important to me was the continuation of a reconstruction I had always fought you on. In the dream you obviously stand for my father. His avoidance of me, his depression (and mine) and door closing is related to his guilt about breaking a sexual taboo. In some way, I am responsible. As painful as the unraveling has been, I'm also quite excited. Obviously, there is a part of me that is identified with you, so that the process continues. The work goes on. I'm even curious at times about what the next chapter will bring.

I thought you would be pleased to know this. You were and continue to be my teacher.

Love,

Bonnie

As discussed in another chapter, by the end of an analysis the patient should feel free during the sessions to say anything that comes to mind, no matter how embarrassing, unimportant, or painful. As Dr. Hyman Spotnitz once said to me, "The more the ego loves itself, the better one is able to free associate." We hope that during the course of an analysis the patient has learned that there is a lot about himself that is lovable, and that whatever he might say or think, essentially he is a decent human being much like everyone else. Unfortunately, we live in the world of reality, and not everyone follows this philosophy.

It is vital that the patient learn when *not* to say everything that comes to mind. It took close to a catastrophe to teach me this when I was a patient. I must have been stupid, and certainly experienced a lapse in judgment, but I was in love with my analyst and with analysis and thought that what was appropriate in analysis probably would work well in the outside world too. At that time I was studying for my doctorate at Columbia University. As I later found out, one of my teachers was very antianalysis. I was foolish enough to challenge his beliefs in class, highlighting what I considered the superiority of analysis to other forms of psychology. The result was disastrous. The professor ignored me completely ever after. Later in my career, he was selected to serve on the committee for my oral examinations. Luckily, the man had enough integrity to decline, or I may never have received the Ph.D. I proudly carry after my name.

I have also indicated that it is highly desirable, if not a necessity, that the former analysand find a mate or a close friend with whom he may experience the same freedom of expression he had in analysis and know his friend will understand that he is simply human. It is especially important to be able to express anger or annoyance to one's confidant; otherwise it mounts up inside like steam, which will explode without a satisfactory outlet.

The person who serves as a confidant to partially replace the analyst is often a surprising choice. This was never more true than in the case of Steven Scott, who was a charming young man of twenty-two when he came to me for analysis. His major problem was his cold, uncaring father, who had seemed disinterested in Steve from the moment he was born. His parents had divorced when he was quite young, and there was very little contact as a family after that. True, Mr. Scott would join his three children on formal occasions such as graduations, but he seemed to attend out of a sense of duty rather than love and exhibited little if any feeling for his offspring. Steve's two siblings long ago had given up hope that their father could ever be a "real" parent. But Steve never stopped hoping. This obsession with his father kept him from settling down in his chosen field of work. His need to please his father shaped his character, as it does with many boys. Steve appeared to be a lovable, appealing young man, although he himself did not believe it to be so. Mr. Scott had been remarried for years, and it was particularly painful for Steve to see his stepmother treated with the care and consideration he sought for himself.

"Why can't he love me that way, too?" he mourned. Steve was truly pathetic as he expressed his lifelong love for his father. Between sobs he described the cruel manner in which his father cut him off and rejected any emotional contact. "All my life I've waited for him to love me," he said, "and he never would."

Suddenly Steve stopped speaking. Then with a surge of insight, he said, "I really haven't tried to get through to him any more than he has to me. I have taken him at his word and suffered his absence in silence. Do you know what? I'm just like *him*. Perhaps I should give him another chance and tell him how I feel."

"Why not?" I answered, not wanting to discourage him, but secretly feeling it was hopeless.

"I'm going to visit him this weekend," Steve said, with a new determination in his voice. "I'll let you know what happens."

I thought about Steve and his mission that weekend, and worried that it was doomed to disappointment. "His father's character cannot possibly change at his age," I thought. "After a lifetime of being withdrawn and remote, how can he be different now?" But it seemed I had underrated the power of Steve and of psychoanalysis.

He came to his next session with a spring in his walk and a note of excitement in his voice. "You cannot imagine what happened this weekend," he said. "*I* cannot imagine it! I got over being scared of my father and decided to tell it to him like it is. He was sitting by the fireplace, looking at the fire and smoking his pipe alone. I went in and sat at his feet. We didn't say anything for a while as we watched the flames together. Then, still watching the fire, I started to talk. I spoke slowly at first, and then it all tumbled out. I told him how much I love him and how I've always needed him; that it's been the tragedy of my life that we haven't been able to be close. Then I looked up at him for the first time that evening.

"I still can't believe what I saw!" he continued. "My father seemed so shocked he couldn't answer. Then he started to cry. After a while, he started talking, too. He said, 'I didn't know, I didn't know! I always thought you preferred your mother and weren't interested in me at all! It was always very painful for me to see the two of you together and think that you were close to her and not to me. I never realized you loved me and needed me to love you. I've *always* loved you but stayed away because I didn't want to be hurt anymore.' Then we threw our arms around each other and both of us cried."

Steve sat silent for a moment, reliving the most important moment of his life. Then he said simply, "I'm very grateful. You've made it possible for me to be open with my father. I have what I've always wanted now. I know my father loves me."

The two men became close after that and saw each other weekly. Because he knew he had his father's love, Steve was able to stop pursuing him in his mind and to devote himself to his career.

Steve's rapprochement with his father happened a long time ago but remains one of the most moving incidents in my forty years of practice. The sequel is equally touching.

Steve has done remarkably well over the years, becoming a famous and wealthy man in his field, on the periphery of the arts. He is an exceptionally endearing fellow; one can see why he was able to pierce through the frosty defenses of his father. I must admit he got to me, too, and is one of my all-time favorite patients. From time to time I was pleased to receive a card from him telling me of his latest successes, or simply saying hello. Recently, however, he called me. After some banter from him about how I was doing and my life in Key West, I detected a strained note in his voice. I immediately stopped joking and said, "What's the matter, Steve?"

"My father is dead," he said, his voice breaking. "It is horrible, horrible, horrible."

I waited until he could talk.

It seems his father developed cancer and was in the terminal stages. He was in great pain and no longer able to go about his life in a way that had any meaning. Steve was vacationing in Europe and received a phone call from his father unlike any he had ever had from him before. Mr. Scott asked his son to come home immediately. Steve dropped everything and flew back that evening.

When he got there, his father had a request. He couldn't go on living anymore. He wanted to shoot himself and asked Steve's help. He said there was no one else he would ask. Steve understood. He in no way tried to dissuade his father, but simply inquired if there wasn't another way that would be less catastrophic. But Mr. Scott had his mind set on the gun. He wasn't even strong enough to sit up in his chair and requested that Steve tie him and the gun in the proper position so that he could do the job right. He then requested Steve to send his stepmother out of the house and stay with him while he killed himself. With his last words he told Steve that the thing he was most proud of in his whole life was his relationship with his son, and that he loved him beyond anyone else on earth. "You are my best friend," he said. Then through blinding tears Steve watched his father pull the trigger.

Steve retched as he described the scene after the bullet went through his father's head. "Bits of his brain and skull were blown yards away, and the entire room was splattered with blood. I wanted to scour the mess but didn't know if I was capable of doing it. The police came and told me to let the undertaker do the cleaning up, but I told myself it was the last thing

I could ever do for my father. I needed to do it myself. Then I cleaned up every bit left of my father's brain and bone.

"I was honored," he said with pride, "that my father trusted me enough to carry out his last wish."

Another patient who experienced an unexpected rapprochement with her parents, in this case dead ones, was Ellie, a woman in analysis with me for many years. She was the child of immigrant parents whom she had never loved or respected. She refused to acknowledge them as significant human beings with anything to teach her, and she sought more satisfactory surrogate parents to model herself after. She was particularly dissatisfied with her mother, who had spent an impoverished life keeping house. Ashamed of the humble origins of her parents, she fabricated imaginary backgrounds for them, to the extent of elevating her father, who was a menial laborer, to the rank of university professor. She rejected her parents so deeply that she had buried almost all memories of childhood. She further distanced herself from her family by taking on an assumed name.

Although Ellie had made much progress in many ways, she left therapy without any change in the internal relations with her parents. Daughters need to identify with their mothers in order to be able to establish selves in their own right. So I was dissatisfied with this aspect of her analysis. But as I felt the early damage she suffered had been too great to allow further development in this area, I agreed to the termination.

Half a year later, Ellie called for an appointment. I rarely know in advance in such cases whether patients need to return to treatment, or merely wish reassurance that they are progressing nicely by themselves. Therefore I was looking forward to seeing her and to hearing how she was doing. To my surprise she walked into the room with a smile on her face, instead of her customary grim expression. We greeted each other with pleasure as she sat down on the chair opposite me, rather than taking her former position on the couch.

"Guess what I just did?" she asked, showing excitement in her usually low voice.

"Tell me," I said. For I had not the slightest idea.

"I registered my parents at Ellis Island, where their names will be memorialized in bronze," she said. "But best of all, I listed my mother in her maiden name. I gave her the identity apart from housekeeper I always wanted her to have. I had thought of her before as a born loser, and who wants to be like a loser?

"I've been working on it," she said. Then, looking me in the eye, she added, "I found out that my mother had a self, so now I can have one, too."

Still another postanalytic solution was experienced by Olga, a middle-aged woman who discovered a talent she really never knew she had. Olga was a very depressed, plump alcoholic when she first entered the consultation room. She had immigrated from Lithuania when she was a young teenager and felt very alone in this country. Her husband had abandoned her to live with a younger woman. Her children had grown up and left home, and she got on with them very badly. In desperation, she had tried a brief involvement with a man of vastly inferior social class, but it had ended badly.

Olga felt hopeless, estranged from the few friends she had by her dreary outlook and incessant complaining. She loathed her job of teaching English as a second language, but continued in it because she didn't know what else to do. She arrived at her first session with hair unkempt and clothes obviously thrown together without effort. She felt comfortable, she admitted, only when she was alone. "My only friend is vodka," she said poignantly.

I was greatly worried about Olga, for she spoke constantly of her joyless existence and the wish to kill herself. Since alcoholism is a form of slow self-destruction, I knew these were not idle threats.

She had been an attractive woman who had derived her sense of self-hood largely from the attention of men. Since the loss of her husband and then a lover, the encroachment of middle age, and the advent of an almost paralyzing depression, Olga believed men no longer sought her out or were interested in her. This drove her even deeper into despair.

Realistically, she had many things to mourn. They included the destruction of her marriage, the estrangement of her children, the loss of male company and the sexual gratification it provided, the end of her youth, and her fading beauty and sexual identity. This mourning process continued several years as she lay on the couch engulfed in misery.

But there were infantile sources of her melancholia as well. Gradually she came to realize that her present losses revived painful memories of childhood. She was able to grieve for parents and siblings long gone and her lost homeland, as well as growing up alone in a strange country.

Then slowly, very slowly, as most therapy progresses, Olga started to change. She ceased drinking and joined Alcoholics Anonymous, where she attended daily meetings. There she made new friends who were available around the clock. She now took an interest in what she wore and joined a health club and began to lose weight. It was touch and go for a while, but finally the new regime prevailed and became a permanent part of her life.

She found and expressed pleasure in a little boutique specializing in colorful "recycled" clothes. Here she could save money as well as enjoy her purchases. I was surprised to find that underneath her former sloppiness lay a unique ethnic style of dressing. She was reconnecting with the person she felt she really was, a little immigrant girl from Lithuania alone in a foreign land. She then was able to build a new identity based on her own inner world. This image replaced the reflections discovered in the eyes of men and made Olga a far more independent person. Instead of seeing herself as "Harold's wife," "Robert's girlfriend," or "Judy and Michael's mother," she now had an image of herself as a courageous, successful person.

She also discovered she "loved" her teaching job, as she helped new Americans to feel at home in this country. And almost imperceptibly, she found herself relating to her own children in a less needy manner. Now they could respond with needs of their own, not to the demands of a desperate mother.

Her self-derogation had ceased. She stood up straighter and was proud of her accomplishments. She admitted, "I like myself more than I ever did, and my children now treat me with love and respect."

Toward the end of her analysis, a completely new career emerged. To everyone's surprise, including her therapist's, Olga turned out to be very talented. She had enrolled at a summer writers' program at Barnard College and discovered she could express on paper the thoughts she previously had denied. Her teacher and fellow students were fascinated with her stories of life in Lithuania, which also were instrumental in completing her mourning for "home."

She did not wish to leave analysis, but finally worked up the courage to try it on her own. Several months later she wrote that she had sold several stories to magazines and was now in the process of writing her first novel. Of course the background of the book was growing up in Lithuania. She said she was deeply involved in the writing and that the experience was more wonderful than she had ever believed possible. I will be very surprised if the book does not turn out to be an enormous success.

Merton Boyle was another very sick patient whose life was changed by immersion in a new career. Merton came to me for analysis when he was twenty-three years old. He had been hospitalized for thirteen months, four years before, for a condition diagnosed as "Dementia praecox, catatonic type." He was brought to the hospital by his father and two attendants, following a period of preoccupation, withdrawal, and a suicidal threat. Merton himself felt that his main difficulty was in relating to his feelings and his emotional relationships with people. He floated on the surface of life, equidistant from friends and family. The hospital report described him as confused and withdrawn, and added, "He was, and has been, remarkably inarticulate for a boy of his background and general intelligence."

He came for analysis because he was failing in school, where he was studying chemistry, a field he had felt pushed into by his chemist father. Merton was not interested at all in chemistry and had no wish to learn about it. In his analysis, we came to the conclusion that his illness was part of a constructive adolescent rebellion against parental authority. This represented a real growth for him.

The turning point in his analysis, and indeed, in his life, came a year or two later when he had a very beautiful dream. In it he was sifting through the various layers of the earth, which were radiantly colored, rather like the Grand Canyon. The dream was extremely sensual, and he could actually feel and smell the soil.

When he spoke about examining the different strata of the earth, Merton said, with unusual enthusiasm, "I'd like to really do that!" That there are other meanings to the dream wish is obvious, but I was happy to stay with its manifest content and the enthusiasm it engendered in him. He may well have understood the dream without my interpretation, for shortly thereafter he got married.

About the same time, Merton changed his major to geology, which he then pursued with great delight and success. I don't know what has happened to him since, because he soon left analysis feeling he no longer needed it or me. But I expect he now is happily and constructively ensconced in his new career as a geologist.

There are other means, besides a one-to-one relationship, of finding freedom of expression before an uncritical audience. For example, some postanalysands have found similar relief and support in a leaderless discussion group. I attend such a weekly gathering in Key West. It consists largely of older women, many of whom have been in analysis or therapy. The members bring a bag lunch and meet for two hours in the garden of one of the group. It is amazing how open, unguarded, and honest most of the speakers are able to be. It is as if their therapy and their life experiences have freed them from the necessity of deceiving themselves or of impressing others.

To exemplify the spirit of the pioneer women who met in quilting bees, each speaker of the group, when finished, passes a small quilted heart to the next person. A different topic is chosen for discussion each session. At the last meeting, the theme of the day was, "What are your passions and your fears?" The idea came to one member who had read about a tribe of Native Americans who held similar meetings, which apparently kept them in good mental health.

The discussion proceeded around a circle, as each member in turn revealed her deepest thoughts and feelings on both her passions and her fears. In many instances the speakers became quite profound and spoke eloquently on matters they care about. Some were activists who fervently fought for causes such as peace and social justice. Other passions varied from that of one woman in remission from cancer who simply wanted to stay alive to that of an artist whose heart's desire was to paint "one great picture" before she died. The major fears expounded were fear of death, of being helpless, dependent, and alone in old age, and of losing one's identity as one grew older. Other important subjects brought up ranged from what it is like to live with cancer, what happens to relationships with children as people age, the loss of idealism, and how people change as a result of the aging process.

Here the postanalysands have replaced the listening analyst with a peer group who is accepting, sympathetic, and non-judgmental. It is also very broadening to hear the deep-seated revelations of people from many walks of life, an experience patients do not get in analysis. I joined the group in order to make new friends, but have found the process of sharing dreams, hopes, and fears with a group of equals extremely therapeutic.

Like my peer group, support groups of many kinds have become invaluable to many postanalysands. One delightfully honest young man, Louis Lee, has been a manic depressive since he was eighteen years old. He feels that analysis was extremely helpful to him, particularly in coping with the disastrous effects of his manic states, and contributed to his remaining symptom free for many years. Nevertheless, Louis regularly attends the Manic and Depressive Support Group in New York City.

He says, "Sometimes when I want to talk about how it feels to be a manic depressive, nobody but a person who suffers from the same illness will understand. No matter how sensitive someone may be in other ways, if he hasn't been through the experience himself, it doesn't feel the same."

Perhaps the most successful and best known of the many types of support groups is Alcoholics Anonymous, a marvelous organization that has served the needs of alcoholics since it was founded in 1935 by Dr. Robert Holbrook Smith and Bill W. to help conquer their own desperate drinking problems. Alcoholics Anonymous is perhaps the most notable of all therapies in leading to the "cure" and to the maintenance of sobriety. As many as 75 percent of those who first wrote their stories in the original edition of *Alcoholics Anonymous* achieved sobriety, and most of those still alive have been sober for an average of twenty years. It is estimated that Dr. Bob, as he was called, along with his cofounder Bill W., guided some five thousand fellow alcoholics to recovery during his fifteen years of loving ministry before his death in 1950.

The American Medical Association, in its booklet "The Illness Called Alcoholism," states:

> The American Medical Association and the World Health Organization, as well as many other professional groups, regard alcoholism as a disease. The judiciary and law-makers also are recognizing it as a disease.
>
> Some authorities continue to see alcoholism only as an expression of underlying emotional problems. Others see it starting as a symptom which precedes an illness and requires treatment in itself.

The latter is the opinion of the late great expert on alcoholism, Dr. Ruth Fox, whom I consulted early in my career about an alcoholic patient. Doctor Fox informed me that alcoholism really is two diseases. According to her, there is an emotional illness that originally leads to drinking, and the physical insatiability that is chemically caused. As they say in A.A., "One drink is too many, but twenty are not enough." To treat an alcoholic, both the physical and emotional illnesses must be addressed.

For this reason, alcoholism is different from other emotional illnesses. Most of us who have been through analysis can afford a psychological slip, for who is seriously hurt if a food binger regresses and eats three candy bars one night? What great harm is done if an obsessional neurotic has a recurrence of his symptom, which he then can analyze away? But it is a different story for the alcoholic; he cannot afford a slip, for his chemical craving can take him right back to where he started. It is for this reason that even successfully analyzed alcoholics continue to need support all their lives. Psychotherapeutic treatment is not enough. Alcoholics Anonymous alone deals with the physical, emotional, and spiritual aspects of the illness.

When the need arises for psychological services that are beyond the ability of A.A. to provide, the basic A.A. textbook, *Alcoholics Anonymous*, initially prepared by a hundred or so alcoholics who had learned to stay sober by helping each other, specifically recommends seeking out such help. They find no conflict between A.A. ideas and the advice of a professional with expert understanding of alcoholism.

Perhaps the best description of what A.A. is and does is expressed in the preamble, usually read at the beginning of every meeting.

> Alcoholics Anonymous is a fellowship of men and women who share their experience, strength and hope with each other that they may solve their common problem and help others to recover from alcoholism.
>
> The only requirement for membership is a desire to stop drinking. There are no dues or fees for A.A. membership; we are self-supporting through our own contributions.
>
> A.A. is not allied with any sect, denomination, politics, organization or institution; does not wish to engage in any controversy; neither endorses nor opposes any causes.
>
> Our primary purpose is to stay sober and help other alcoholics to achieve sobriety.

There are more than seventy-three thousand A.A. groups worldwide, and all members are free to attend any meeting anywhere of A.A. This factor alone is therapeutic; members never have to feel a stranger anywhere in the world, as there are always local meetings he or she can attend and be assured of a warm welcome. When I first moved to Key West and didn't know many people, I told an alcoholic friend (only half in jest) that I wished I were an alcoholic so I could find fifty instant friends!

At meetings, members discuss their own drinking experiences before coming into the organization and explain how A.A. principles led them to sobriety and a new outlook on life. The experiences of Nan Nesbit, a recovered alcoholic, whom I heard speak at a meeting, are discussed at length in a later chapter. Older members like Nan try to help newcomers and each other, and are available around the clock. The ready accessibility of members to one another is another therapeutic asset that is essential to the recovery of some patients and is not generally available anywhere but in hospitals.

Meetings are informal and usually include friendly get-togethers around the coffee table. Visitors are impressed with the laughter and general atmosphere of good humor and warm fellowship at the meetings. Members generally take their illness seriously, but not themselves. Part of the recovery process is finding the ability to laugh about experiences that once brought tears.

Few people are aware that A.A. had its beginnings in the office of the great psychoanalyst Carl Jung. Dr. Jung was talking to Mr. R., a prominent American businessman who had gone the typical alcoholic route. Medicine and hospitalization had left his addiction untouched, and he came for treatment to Dr. Jung as a last resort. Dr. Jung treated Mr. R. for a year, until the patient felt that he understood the compulsion that had led him to drink. Nevertheless, he found himself drunk shortly after leaving the care of Dr. Jung.

Mr. R. returned to Dr. Jung in a state of black despair and asked what else he could possibly do to find a cure. Dr. Jung pessimistically answered that medicine had done all it could for Mr. R. and those alcoholics whose illness was as severe.

"Is there no exception? Is this the end of the line for me?" Mr. R. shouted.

Dr. Jung replied that here and there he had known a few exceptions, alcoholics who had had vital spiritual experiences, in the nature of huge emotional displacements and rearrangements. These people were able to discard old patterns of thinking and establish a whole new set of principles. The doctor continued that ordinary religious faith isn't enough, that what he was talking about was a transforming experience, a conversion.

He suggested that Mr. R. place himself in the religious atmosphere of his choice, recognize his personal hopelessness, and cast himself on whatever god he thought there was. "The lightning of the transforming experience of conversion may then strike you," continued the great physician. Dr. Jung's words struck Mr. R. at great depth and it was a humbling experience. Today deflation at depth remains a cornerstone principle of A.A. The basis of this principle is that the alcoholic must accept the fact that he or she is powerless over alcohol and other people, places, and things and that there is a higher power to whom he or she must submit.

Mr. R. joined the Oxford Group of the day as his religious group and became quite active in it. To his intense joy and surprise, the obsession to drink presently left him.

Once when Bill W. was lost in the deepest depression he had ever known, a friend told him about Mr. R.'s conversion. Bill cried out that he was ready to try anything and shrieked, "If there be a God, will he show himself!" To his astonishment, the room lit up in a flash of blinding light. Bill felt ecstasy, as though he were on a mountaintop. A great wind blew, enveloping and penetrating him. There came the blazing thought, "You are a free man." One with the universe, a great peace stole over him. After considerable reading, Bill set out to cure other alcoholics.

A short while later he met Dr. Bob, who was still drinking. The two men immediately understood each other. When Dr. Bob heard about Bill's experiences, he sobered almost immediately. The idea of mutual need added the final ingredient to the synthesis of medicine, religion, and the alcoholic experience that is now Alcoholics Anonymous.

Numerous support groups are available today for all sorts of illnesses and emotional difficulties: Al-Anon for family members of alcoholics, the nationwide Manic and Depressive Support Group, Narcotics Anonymous, Overeaters Anonymous, Weight Watchers, Gamblers Anonymous, Smokenders, Shoplifters Anonymous, AIDS groups, Obsessive Compulsives, groups for the families of the emotionally ill, "Tough Love," for parents of addicted teenagers, Mothers Against Drunk Driving (MADD), groups for the survivors of rape, groups for those individuals who have lost a loved one through murder, Parents Without Partners, Alzheimer's disease and cancer support systems for both victims of the diseases and their families, and groups that help sufferers to deal with grief and dying. These are only some of the many groups that exist for the purpose of giving emotional and intellectual support to those in need.

Before leaving the topic of support groups, I would like to distinguish between mutual help or support groups and group therapy. While some groups such as A.A. are often of help to severely disturbed individuals, by and large, members of mutual-support groups are emotionally healthy people who are seeking to cope with their feelings at a stressful and painful period of their lives. The groups often help these individuals to meet their pressing needs in practical ways and make the necessary adjustments to a new and difficult phase of their lives. The support groups help members cope with pain, frustration, loss, and anger, but these members are rarely people who are paralyzed by their life situations. Their egos, identities, self-esteem, and characters are relatively intact. This is in contrast to many of those who enter therapy suffering from emotional illness. That is why support groups often are ideal for people who have completed analysis.[1]

I have given a number of examples of ways in which various patients have filled the void left by analysis. But the definitive answer to the question of what takes the place of analysis can only be answered by the character of the individual patient. Every person is different, as confirmed by fingerprints and handwriting specimens. Every writer, every artist, every composer has something unique to say. Similarly, every patient who terminates will do something different with his life. A good analogy is how one spends an inheritance. My own children and I are a good example of this. When my husband died, each member of the family was left a certain amount of money. Each of us spent it differently. Our oldest child, a dedicated numismatist, invested a good deal of his windfall in coins. Our daughter spent hers going to graduate school. And our younger son bought his future wife a stunning engagement ring. I spent mine on a house. So it is with the extra energy one is left with on the successful completion of analysis.

Former patients have chosen to spend their psychoanalytic inheritance in many ways. In my case, the picture has changed as the years go on. The first result was that I became my own analyst. I had been recording my own dreams since I was twenty-one years old, but after my formal analysis ended, I began to work on them in earnest. I did not let go of them until I felt they were understood, particularly if they referred to a patient. Fortunately, although untrained in analysis, my husband was quite good at divining the meaning of dreams. By discussing them with him, I frequently would come to the feeling encoded in the dream. Once I had a particularly troubling dream that I didn't understand. I went to consult with one of the world's great analysts about it. I came away from the meeting with a new fund of invaluable knowledge. The man didn't even charge for the session. I have never forgotten either his wisdom or his kindness.

In another use of my new psychoanalytic "fortune," I literally became the analyst. When I first terminated analysis, the loss of my analyst left an empty space inside. Relationships with patients soon began to fill the hole. I had deeply valued the relationship with her and unconsciously tried to reproduce it in my practice. I now was the analyst and found in many patients a dissatisfied child. Like my analyst, at times I could be loving, understanding, accepting. Then I could enjoy vicariously what I myself had wanted. The mothering "cured" much suffering, as the warmth of my analyst had "cured" me. (For who is there among us who has been mothered enough?)

By discovering what was important to me, I was able to simplify my life. I now had more time and energy to throw myself into my career. My commitment deepened. In two years I doubled my practice. I took on more difficult patients and tried to learn along with them how they needed to be treated. I read more, studied more, went for further supervision. I also found time to do some research on mothers and children under the guidance of the famed psychoanalyst Margaret Mahler. This research resulted in my first professional publication.[2] I was in my thirties when I finished analysis. By the end of it, I had worked out the following life goals: At age forty I will be the best analyst I possibly can become; by the time I am fifty, I will know enough to begin to write about what I have learned. And to the best of my knowledge that is just what has happened.

I was already married with children by the time I finished analysis. I like to think that my treatment changed my relationship with each member of the family for the better, including the one with my husband, who found me easier to get along with. It is hard to define exactly how I was different, for I believe analysis imperceptibly transformed me in ways I am still discovering. For example, when my very masculine son said to me he really was very much like me, I was incredulous, for I had always thought he was just like his father. When I asked him how he resembled me, I was touched to hear him answer, "I am tender to my wife the way you were to me." I also can see my own contribution to the personalities of my other two children in the ways they bring up their own youngsters. Then I am especially grateful that I had the advantage of psychoanalysis.

Shortly after my analysis was over, I became very friendly with another of my analyst's ex-patients. Just as early in my life my older sister took over part of the role of my mother, my friend adopted some of the functions of our ex-analyst. I believe I did the same for her. This friend is a very accepting person, which makes her a fine analyst indeed. It was particularly valuable to me that, as with my own analyst, there was nothing I could say to her that she wouldn't understand. I used to joke that if I told her, "I just killed my mother," her response could only be, "I'm sure you had good reason."

In this new era of my life, the force of energy I once devoted to analysis, and before that to neurosis, is now focused on my writing career. I feel it is fueled by exactly the same source of power. We only have so much of it; if it is going to go into conflict, it is unavailable for work. I much prefer to have this force to dispense with as I consciously wish.

Some will spend this energy enriching their family life, others in deepening their knowledge of the interest of their choice. Some may change their careers altogether. Still others may buy themselves the time and leisure to travel. Some become activists or deeply involved in a cause. It is always interesting for the analyst to see how the freshly analyzed patient will spend his psychological inheritance. But whatever the choice the individual makes, there is one fact I am sure of: His life will be infinitely richer and deeper than it ever was before.

8

Life after Analysis: Three Diverse Paths

The three women to be discussed in this chapter are Ruth Dreamdigger, dream specialist; Frances Froelicher, noted social activist; and Nan Nesbit,[1] a woman who uses the support group of Alcoholics Anonymous to help herself and others stay well. The women, all of whom live or vacation in Key West, illustrate three different avenues taken by people who have successfully terminated psychoanalytic treatment.

Ruth Dreamdigger, Dreamer of Dreams

Ruth Dreamdigger is a woman whose creativity was released through her treatment. Perhaps of the three people to be described, she comes closest to having completely replaced psychoanalysis in her life. She does it largely through her understanding of dreams, which she uses in the workshops she leads, as well as for her own self-understanding.

When asked to be interviewed for this book, Ruth was most amenable and happy to be of assistance. She is a small, wide-eyed woman of perhaps seventy, with omnipresent round glasses and a Buster Brown cut to her gray hair. The influence of the Women's Movement is reflected in her casual, braless style of dressing. A gentle, quiet soul, with a sweet disposition, her strong beliefs come as a surprise to the chance observer.

She began to speak as soon as the interviewer sat down.

"Like most people I used to think that dreams were unimportant," she said. "It was just a dream, so it never occurred to me there was anything to learn from it. It was definitely analysis that started me in this direction. I began it, because of a dream, almost as soon as I became an adult.

"I had led a very unsocial and withdrawn life until I came to New York and stayed at a place called Labor Temple. It was run by the Presbyterian church and had been a center for solving labor relations problems. When I got there, it was more of a meeting place for almost any unpopular group. The Trotskyites, the Russian church pacifists, met there. It was an interracial group, and there were about a dozen of us in it. It was the first time in my life that it was possible to think and say anything at all—where nothing I said would be too shocking. Liberation came out of that. In this atmosphere I sort of blossomed and for the first time in my life became popular with men. Of course I was delighted and felt pretty much on the top of the world.

"I began having a dream of a herd of elephants tramping over me." Ruth looked at the writer significantly, and we both laughed. She continued, "I didn't know a thing about dreams. Oddly enough it was not a nightmare. It says it all, doesn't it, but I didn't know it then. I just thought it was an odd dream.

"And then I dreamed that I was on a sofa asleep, and it began to tip over, and up behind the back of it came a disembodied hand. Like in the Addams family. They call it The Thing. But mine wasn't funny; it was true nightmare material. I started screaming and woke myself and everybody else up. At that point one of the men who had been my lover told me I'd better see a therapist. He said he had just the therapist for me, and his name was Rollo May. He was a very young man then (it was 1944) with, I think, two children, and he practiced in his home. I was working for the Socialist party and had practically no money, and he let me see him for seven-and-a-half dollars a session. I was very lucky to have found him.

"I come from a religious fundamentalist family and had a lot of guilt about all the sexual activity I was having. I was bursting with life, passion, and energy, and he helped me accept the essence of myself. We did much of this through dreams.

"The analysis ended when I got married, and I didn't go back for several years. By then I had learned a lot about my feelings from dreams. But after I had a few kids, I realized I still was very neurotic. Once I had spent the entire day saying under my breath, 'Stupid, stupid, stupid!' So I went to a woman therapist and continued on and off for a number of years. She was very good with dreams, too. I continued with her until I went to Philadelphia in 1973. It was there I decided I probably would never be able to afford therapy again, so I better begin using my dreams myself.

"At first I tried reading Freud and Jung. But I soon realized I couldn't learn that way. It just wasn't working. Then Ann Faraday's book *Dream Power* came out, and it was in everyday language. I realized that you *can* do it yourself, that you just need to learn new work habits.

"I was in a community then called Movement for a New Society, a kind of a radical, pacifist, society-changing group. We did a lot of workshops on sexism, racism, homophobia, classism, all of the oppressions. The community believed that the personal and the political must go together in order to have a good society of people who are mentally healthy.

"In Philadelphia I had even less money than before because I was involved in this social-action movement and couldn't afford analysis. Actually, a few years later I broke my hip, and that brought up a lot of fear that I was going to be dependent. I became terribly depressed and had to go back for more therapy. My young woman therapist put her finger on the problem immediately. When I was fourteen my mother had died, and I became dependent on people who wanted to be kind but could not deal with my problems. It was really a dreadful time, and the idea of ever being dependent on anybody again threw me.

"But because I was in this group where personal growth was important along with social change, it was easy for me to find a group of compatible women. Mainly I worked with women who wanted to join me in a quest of what our dreams were telling us. This circle stayed together for many years, telling each other our dreams. Although the personnel of the group changed a good deal, at the end of thirteen years, two of the original members were still in it. It was very exciting and helpful to me. We all became very good at recognizing symbols and became very supportive of each other. I remember one time I had a dream that was very painful. All of a sudden one of the members said, 'You know, Ruth, it's all right to cry in dream group.' I burst into tears.

"It was a peer group; nobody led it. We just kind of winged it, learning as we went along.

"Then, for health reasons I had to move down here to Key West. I realized how important the dream group had been for my well-being and decided to try to form a similar one. In the community in which I live I had a readymade bunch of people who would support me. We began a dream group, and it worked much as the first one had. We have been meeting once a week for about five years now. I'm not a leader in this group, either.

I don't want to be.[2] It hadn't occurred to me that I would ever use this skill professionally.

"There is something else along the lines of mental health that I have been doing for many years. It is called peer counseling. I am a grassroots person and like to do things myself. I met a woman who was interested in doing peer counseling with me who does not live in the community. I sort of trained her to do this kind of work, and we each counsel the other. We've also done it for about six years and have become a great support to each other.

"A few years ago I was very strapped for money. She led me to believe I could make a little money in what I've learned about dreams. It took me a long time to believe it. But now I have this little business, a dream workshop here or there, an occasional dream consultation. I go to New York twice a year to visit my family. I have a lot of friends there. Quite often when I'm there, one of my friends will organize a workshop for me. This year I'm going to do a workshop there at a new place, a woman's organization called the Crystal Quilt. Down here I do them at the Blue Moon Trader on Big Pine and the Island Wellness Center in Key West.

"The way it works is really very simple. Someone in the group volunteers to read a dream or tell it. If the dreamer has any ideas of what it might mean, she says so. Then the rest of us put in any thoughts we might have. It is up to the dreamer to decide whether the input she has gotten feels right to her. Sometimes if we still don't know what the dream is about, we will use the object of 'I am.'[3] Then we just go around the circle. We've been together so long now that the dream will bring up many other subjects. It's a very loose framework. It means that sometimes the meetings go on for a very long time.

"When I start out with a new group, the first half of the meeting I ask the participants what experience they've had with dreams, if they have read anything useful, if they have recurrent dreams or nightmares, whether there is anything in particular they are interested in exploring. Then we have a discussion based on the input. In all, the workshops usually take three hours. In the second half we work on the dreams themselves. Then we just proceed with the Gestalt system.

"There are a lot of people who come to dream workshops who feel they have had psychic experiences. I tell them my belief that dreams operate on three levels. To some extent this is Ann Faraday's thinking.

"If on the first level, for example, I trip on a carpet, I might check out whether the carpet really has a loose thread. Sometimes a dream will give that sort of useful practical information.

"Level two is one of feelings. The dream is telling us how we feel. That's the level I work at the most.

"Then there is level three, that of telepathy and precognition, which does seem to operate; I can't discount it. We definitely enter each other's dreams. My daughter and I had a dream that was exactly the same although we were behaving very differently at the time. If someone believes she is talking with her dead mother, I don't try to discourage her. What I do say is that we all have internalized the people who raised us, and if I dream of my mother, it is the mother who still lives in me I am dreaming of and not necessarily the real mother at all.

"The reality is that the groups have helped a lot of people, and that makes me feel very good. I also point out to people the use of puns in our dreams, that sometimes we use the names of people as puns, and that sometimes we'll turn them around. I had one recently in which I was beating a drum around a bush. I'm not an admirer of George Bush, and knew I would not be beating the drum for him. It suddenly occurred to me that *I* was beating around the bush. I knew immediately in what circumstance I was doing it. That's what I love about dreams. They are often terribly funny.

"I had another a long time ago that still makes me smile. I dreamed there was a monkey on the top of a building, trying to hide behind plumbing pipes. As I worked on the dream, I realized that plumbing to me is represented by the trade name American Standard. Monkeys stand for foolishness. The dream told me that I was trying to hide some foolishness behind high standards. Even if you get information that isn't so easy to deal with, it is usually in a form that makes it easier to handle.

"I try never to use other people's dreams in workshops. Instead I use examples from my own dreams. I want people to feel totally safe with me and to know that there is no way anything I learn about them in dreams will go anywhere else. A woman stopped me on the street the other day. There had been a name she had used in one of her dreams that she didn't recognize. I suggested that if she turned the name around perhaps she could understand it. She did, and it worked. She said it helped her enormously. Many people have told me that the workshops have given them a whole new perspective about who they are and what they could do for themselves."

"How did you get your name?" the interviewer asked.

"As the feminist movement came along, a lot of women were changing their names," she answered. "My married name was Ruth Best. I had never liked it. It seemed very competitive. It also was clear to me that my husband and I were going in separate paths. And I didn't want to go back to my childhood name, because it represented a lot of pain to me.

"Then one morning in May I woke up and the word *dreamdigger* was in my mind. And right away I knew that was for me.

"The process of changing names was really very simple," she continued with a smile. "First I got a library card. Then I went to the bank. Then I got a driver's license. Although that ordinarily would require a notary, I had a friend who did it for me for nothing. From there I went to voting, then to getting a passport. The same with my social security number. So I became, officially, Ruth Dreamdigger with no trouble at all. That amuses me a great deal. I feel sure that everybody in the establishment hierarchy assumed I was marrying Mr. Dreamdigger. But there never was any. I wonder if a man could change his name that easily.

"Another interesting aspect to me is that when I changed my name, in the late seventies, people I was introduced to often would make fun of it. 'Oh, Ruth Gravedigger,' they would say. Or 'Why don't you just say dreamer, if you want to say anything about dreams?' Now the response I get is totally different. It's always 'What an interesting name! What a kind of exciting name! How did you get it?' But it's always with pleasure rather than taunting. That encourages me. It indicates that people are gradually learning to accept differences in society. It's been a long time now since anyone has put me down because of my name.

"There is one thing that is very important to me. At heart I am a social activist. My work with dreams is really connected with that. I feel that in our dreams we learn to be less judgmental. We learn to accept ourselves as human beings, and then we can accept others, too. Much of the pain we inflict on each other both personally and politically is because we do not allow each other to have different ways of being. That's the root of a lot of disharmony, even war."

The Visions of Frances Froelicher

One would never guess in the company of Frances Froelicher that one is in the presence of greatness. Her humility and simplicity of manner belie it. Yet she is a great activist and visionary, one of the most distinguished in the United States. Her efforts have extended to three locations: Baltimore, the Gettysburg area, and Key West. For her contributions she has received two honorary doctorates and considerable national recognition, culminating in 1991 in a ceremony at the White House with President Bush.

A silver-haired, elderly lady, somewhat stooped in stature by now, Dr. Froelicher impressed me as looking the typical WASP she is, her distinguished forebears having come over on the Mayflower. When asked if she had ever been in analysis, she answered that she had.

"I am very allergic to everything," she said, "and I have what's called a spastic colon or an overactive bowel. I got help from a wonderful doctor who was one of the first graduates of The Johns Hopkins School of Medicine. Even when I finished treatment, whenever I had trouble she would say come on out and we'll talk about it. She kept me going for many years. She is still alive; she must be over 100 by now, so I don't go to her anymore. But that's good because I have so little time and can get along without a doctor now. I still have the spastic colon but manage to talk myself out of it."

Dr. Froelicher probably is not aware that she is able to talk herself out of her spastic colon because she was helped by her analysis. The energy formerly invested in her treatment is now allotted to her activism. This became clear as she spoke about her vision for humanity and how she had worked on it in her hometown of Baltimore.

"My niece is a criminal lawyer," she said, "who believes that people's visions activate good things in the world. If you have a vision, then you can work to bring it about. But without a vision nothing can change. For thirty-nine years I had the vision of Baltimore as a slumless city, where people could work together for better housing and the elimination of poverty and racial and religious prejudice. And much of it was accomplished. Now every winter I work to make my vision for Key West come true."

From 1941 to 1969 Dr. Froelicher was professional director of the Baltimore Citizens Planning and Housing Association, a nonprofit citizens organization she founded. The movement emphasizes people power, enlisting volunteers and mobilizing citizens to battle for worthwhile public causes. At its height, there were 500 people involved in 50 committees, 110 people on the board of directors, 3,000 individual members representing every aspect of the community, and 350 civic improvement organizations. CPHA was able to set up many new public agencies and have laws passed instituting new programs. Its members had a major impact on the cleanup and rehabilitation of the city, culminating in what became known as the Baltimore Renaissance. Mainly it was responsible for developing citizen leadership, which resulted in members serving as leaders on many prestigious boards, such as the library and art museums. They became members of the city council and state legislatures and were elected congressmen and senators. Maryland's present senators, Paul Sarbanes and Barbara Mikulski have their roots in the Citizens Planning and Housing Association.

"This is what is so encouraging," Dr. Froelicher continued enthusiastically, "that great things can be accomplished when citizens take power. If citizen power could help change one city, it can do it other places as well."

In 1969 Dr. Froelicher resigned her job as director of the agency, as she felt attitudes had changed and she no longer could be effective. In her twenty-nine years of indefatigable work in the job, she and the CPHA took Baltimore from a city that didn't admit it had any slums to one that adopted housing as an official policy. She and her organization guided the city into the Baltimore Renaissance, rebuilding the harbor and much of the downtown area. She and the CPHA reformed the corrupt housing authority, which was controlled by the real estate interests. They were instrumental in getting three reform commissioners on the housing agency. According to the Baltimore newspaper *The Sun* (July 21, 1991), the face of Baltimore has been changed forever by the efforts of this great lady and her associates.

Not satisfied with working on the revitalization of her hometown, Dr. Froelicher then extended her vision to Fairfield, Pennsylvania, sixty-five miles northwest of Baltimore. She said, "My husband and I discovered the area on our honeymoon thirty years ago and fell in love with it. When he died in 1976, I decided to try to preserve the 519 acres near Gettysburg that we had acquired over a period of thirty years. It is called Strawberry Hill. It is set in the Blue Ridge Mountains and is one of the most scenic spots in the world," she said, her eyes sparkling.

"We had bought a small piece of property, only a quarter of an acre, and fixed it up. It was only an old store with no facilities, and we made it into a lovely little house on the border of a stream. We called it New Hope Cottage. We gradually acquired the 519 acres of stream and forest land, which we bought to safeguard our property.

"Before my husband died, we had made up our minds that it had taken us thirty-five years to develop this beautiful land, and we were going to do our best to protect it. For thirty-five years we used all our skills as citizen facilitators to preserve these 519 acres. We had laid out the trails and rebuilt the houses, so there are now five rental houses on the property in addition to the four used by the center. We successfully fought a large vacation development and a quarry that was polluting our streams. We set up a nonprofit foundation to receive the property as a gift after our deaths, which would eventually be controlled by the local community."

As a result, Strawberry Hill today is a model area, with a historic restored log-and-stone house, two pure streams, which are very unusual in Pennsylvania, and 519 acres of wetlands and forest that have been preserved from encroaching development through environmental-education programs and citizens' action.

The center has been awarded first place three times for the best use of private land in Pennsylvania, as well as in the Take Pride in America contest in 1991. Today several thousand school and youth groups like the Boy Scouts and Girl Scouts make regular use of the property under the guidance of volunteer naturalists that the center trains. Last year the nonprofit center drew 1,400 visitors for nature walks, lectures, and other organized events. It has around 700 members who help support its educational efforts with dues. There is presently a $44,000 budget for 1992, which the group has not yet been able to raise from the community.

"Our project is unique because we are educating children to love the land, fresh air, and water and to protect them as well. Our cities are becoming empty shells, with vacant houses used for drugs and gangs. Cities are the centers of our culture and high technology. If they go to pieces, we are not going to have very much of anything left.

"I'm trying to get people involved in both cities and rural areas to see how the conditions in both are related. Rural people do not see any connection. They just say they won't go to cities because of the criminal element. But they don't understand that the overflow from the cities is destroying the countryside that is unprepared for the tremendous influx that is taking place."

Dr. Froelicher paints with a large palette on a wide canvas indeed. Her vision of making the world a better place extends equally to Key West.

She has owned a house in Key West since 1975 and vacationed there for at least five years before that. She first came there in 1969, when she retired from her job. Her husband died in 1976, when he was eighty-five years old.

"It is very interesting to know he was seventy-one when we married, and he was a great-grandfather," she said with a rare smile. "He was my boss for twelve years at the Citizens Planning and Housing Association, so we had known each other for a long time.

"I have a vision for Key West," she continued. "To me it is a paradise. But it could be much more of a paradise if the various groups here had a deeper understanding of its difficulties and of each other."

Every winter when she comes for her three-month sojourn in Key West, Dr. Froelicher becomes involved in some activity to better the community. She says, "I'm a teacher, so I try to show what has to be done and then leave others to do it. Then I go on to something else."

During one of her "vacations" here, she served as chairman of a cleanup committee of the Key West Garden Club. Another year she worked on mental health and was instrumental in getting two beds for the mentally ill at the hospital. A third time she worked with the Women's Club in connection with the Sands School, which resulted in the installation of a quiet room where disturbed children can be helped to calm down. She also has worked with the League of Women Voters on the issue of water pollution. Always at the cutting edge of progress, she worked on the first ordinance concerning the curtailing of injection wells in this community. She is always involved with the library and on occasion suggests programs on Latin America.

"Since college days I've been interested in Spain and Latin America. As a history major in college, I always felt that English and French were overemphasized, and Spanish, Indian, and Black history neglected.

"When I came to Key West, I was naturally concerned with Cubans and Cuban history," she continued, before discussing her plan to better Cuban American relations. "I have long felt that no adequate history on the contributions of Cubans has been written. One of the greatest attractions of Key West is the Latin American or Cuban atmosphere—the language, the music, the food. It is important that the small-business contributions of Cuban "Key Westers" be documented, like the history of its restaurants, plumbing, and funeral homes. Up to now all Key West histories have been written from a special point of view. For instance, all the tours are of old Bahamian houses, and as far as I know, no Cuban houses are included. The people say there is no Cuban architecture worth seeing, but I feel that no great effort has been made to find it. One tour might just be of what people have done to old Cuban houses like mine. Too many houses down here look like New York apartments."

Then the great activist continued, "If people know more about their history, the Cubans will be prouder of themselves, and others will be proud of them, too. It will bring about better relationships between the groups. I struggle everywhere I go because I am always trying to carry out my visions."

While writing this chapter, the author spent much time reflecting on the psychology of Frances Froelicher. From whence came this child of the privileged classes who has passed so much of her life helping the poor and disadvantaged and working to save the planet for posterity? Why isn't she spending her waning years enjoying the well-deserved fruits of her own, her late husband's, and her distinguished family's labor? Where does this woman of eighty find the energy to work so tirelessly for the good of humanity, in three different areas of the country?

In my opinion, the answer lies in her identity. She is an activist; that is her central core. Anyone who has spent any time in Francis Froelicher's presence knows that her projects occupy her from morning to night, that there is rarely a moment she is not thinking of how she can contribute to some social good.

For example, I recently attended a meeting of the Key West Friends of the Library, where author Jane O'Reilly was to address the audience. Dr. Froelicher arrived early and left late and spent every possible moment including the intermission "working" the room to encourage members of the audience to attend the meeting of a civic group on environmental issues scheduled for that evening. Incidentally, she persuaded the author to attend, too.

All right, you might say. Agreed that this is her identity, can you tell us how she got that way?

I can speculate on the following: Dr. Froelicher informed me that her mother also was an activist, a wonderful community worker who was interested in the church and aging, things that were acceptable in her time.

According to Dr. Froelicher, "I saw what she did in her work, and she inspired me to develop a conscience. Her feeling was noblesse oblige. She felt very strongly that she had more opportunities than most people. Her father had taught her that; he was the mayor of New York and a major in the Civil War in the Battle of Gettysburg. My whole family had a very strong sense of community. My mother was a terrific person. She went to college in Massachusetts from a small town in New York and graduated in 1898 from Smith. That was unheard of at the time."

"You followed in her footsteps," I said.

"Indeed I did," answered the activist. Then she continued, saying that she was often a lonely child, as her mother went about her social activities, leaving the little girl largely in the care of a nurse. The only way for Frances to *have* a mother was to *become* that mother herself. So Frances Froelicher became an activist, too, and mother and daughter were one. As long as she is an activist, she is not a forlorn child. She is never lonely; she is never angry. What greater benefit can analysis achieve than it brought to Frances Froelicher, who has learned to satisfy her deepest needs at the same time she serves mankind?

Nan Nesbit: Conqueror of Addiction

Still another postanalytic path was taken by Nan Nesbit, who won back her health and that of other alcoholics in the support group of Alcoholics Anonymous.

I first saw Nan at an A.A. meeting that I attended with an alcoholic friend. I had never been to such a gathering before. It was an open meeting, and this slight fifty-year-old woman whose weathered face obviously had seen a great deal of life was the speaker of the evening. She spoke well, and her effortless, relaxed quality seemed to be transmitted to her fellow alcoholics, who hung on her every word. I was struck by her honesty and directness, as she spoke without self-pity of her illness and the most intimate, indeed horrible, events of her drinking life. She talked in a spritely, semihumorous, even droll fashion. I felt this ability could only have been achieved after years of mastering the trauma of her illness.

She began by telling of her delight in gulping vanilla straight out of the bottle when she was only six years old. Nobody had noticed, she said, and added that if she saw a child doing such a thing, she would know immediately that the child was an embryo alcoholic. "I still like vanilla," she said impishly.

All through her growing-up years, Nan informed us, she had looked forward to the time she would be able to drink. And indeed, when she took her first drink in the back of a roadster at age sixteen, she immediately got drunk.

"I was on my way home from a junior-achievement meeting with some people who were not in my customary peer group," she said. "They wanted to stop and get some beer, and I just knew that the great moment I'd been waiting for was there. Whee-e-e, it was time to drink! It made me feel great, like I was five-feet-eight inches tall, blond, witty, and sophisticated."

"Alcohol soon consumed me," she continued. "My entire set of friends changed; my ambitions changed. There is a certain well-documented progression to the disease, and with me it advanced with lightning speed in about three to four months. When school interfered with my drinking, I quit school. I spent all my time plotting and scheming how to get hold of liquor. I cultivated friends and structured my activities accordingly. I would go to any kind of occasion where they had liquor, whether I was interested in it or not. And I shunned people who didn't drink. They were boring; they weren't any fun. They didn't know what living was. This was in high school, and it only got worse."

Because of her upbeat charming personality and her skill at manipulating the facts, Nan could always find work easily. But each time, her need for liquor would overcome the wish to be self-sufficient, and she would either quit the job or be fired. Although early in her drinking career Nan was content to drink only in the evenings, she soon found herself so soaked in liquor that "every cell was shot through with alcohol." Thus even when she wasn't drinking, for all practical purposes she was drunk for days at a time.

Frequently her coworkers were what A.A. calls enablers; they pretended not to notice, or were instrumental in helping Nan cover up her inability to function. Her family were even worse enablers; they continued, possibly unwittingly, to give her money to subsist on and for liquor when she was too drunk to hold a job.

She was not a secretive drinker at all and still finds it hard to fathom that her parents were unaware of it. "Many women drinkers are secret closet drinkers, do their drinking at home.

I was not that type. I really didn't really care who knew and who didn't. It doesn't bother me if people approve or disapprove of me, so I didn't care what they thought. And of course when I drank, I was totally defiant. I was sort of bristly all the time, just waiting for someone to criticize me and get on my wrong side. I absolutely adored fighting. I spent my life getting people to be mad so I could fight back. Sometimes just a 'good morning' would do it.

"My second husband and I borrowed a considerable amount of money from my father to buy a business," she continued. "We used the entire amount of the capital to take vacations, to have parties, to live very big with fancy cars and all that, until one day there was just not enough money to carry on the business, and we just shut the doors. I remember sitting upstairs with this huge cardboard box of all the work I hadn't done for years, IRS notices, unfilled orders we had promised and never delivered, and unpaid bills. I just said the hell with it and set it on fire. My thinking must have been that if there were no records, no one could possibly put any blame on me. I remember explaining to my father how it was all my rotten good-for-nothing husband's fault. My father believed me because he wanted to.

"We lived next door to my mother and father. I think they must have had a clue about what was going on, because we weren't quiet. After the business fiasco, would you believe my father hired me to work for him? I proceeded to make merry with his business, too, as a bookkeeper. I carry my share of guilt, but another part of me asks, How could he not notice? How could a four-hundred-dollar-a-month secretary be driving a brand new XKE? The more distance I have on the situation and the less emotional involvement with it, the more I have to say yes, I did a lot of things that were wrong, but how about the guy who let me? In the beginning I was willing to take all the blame, but now I can see that the sickness in the family did not originate with me."

Some of her descriptions were hilarious. She kept much of the audience laughing, as she described one episode after another in which she and her first two husbands got away with deceiving their parents—like the time she fired all of her father's employees and hired her husband and drinking buddies. What she did not realize at the time, of course, was that they were primarily deceiving themselves.

But the recitation was not all amusing; indeed, much of it was appalling. Nan found herself totally unable to function in her life without a drink. For example, one time she became sober and returned to a former job. There she found herself looking at papers as if she had never seen them before, turning them over and over in her hands, as if she were trying to make sense out of hieroglyphics. The liquor helped her relate to people socially, emotionally, and professionally. She says now that she simply didn't know how to be a person without it, that alcohol gave her an identity. Her bizarre, unpredictable, and often unmanageable behavior was the price she felt she had to pay to remain a functioning person.

Intrigued by the pluck and strength of this valiant woman, I approached Nan at the end of the evening and asked if she would consent to an interview. She quickly agreed, saying with disarming candor that she felt flattered by my interest.

We met for lunch several days later. She looked even slighter than I remembered. Casually but nicely dressed, she obviously had made a point of looking her best. She wore an attractive slack suit and completed her ensemble with long dangling earrings and necklace.

As if there had been no interval between her talk and the interview, she immediately picked up her sad but inspiring tale. According to Nan, she had many identities when "under the influence." For example, when she was a young woman, and her second husband was into stock-car racing, she wore bell-bottom jeans and hung around with auto racers. To act out this identity, Nan drank beer. Later she settled on Scotch, which, to her, suggested a business woman of the Ivy League type who wore business suits and carried a portfolio. This seems to be an interesting function of alcohol, made use of by people who do not know who they are when sober.

Nan also had a "happy" identity, when she drank to ward off the effects of drugs like "speed," which she says literally made her insane. She used speed to lengthen the time that she could drink. "Speed is a stimulant, not quite as powerful as crack or cocaine, but it peps you up and keeps you from sleeping," Nan explained. "It keeps you highly energized and tends to offset the depressive cycle of alcohol, where you pass out and can't drink anymore.

"After a binge you may have had a half hour's fun," she continued. "You think, boy I was the life of the party, I danced with everyone, I was the world's greatest lover. There might have been a half hour out of twenty-four that you really enjoyed yourself. But as the disease progresses, there is no period of feeling good and high at all. You feel like your best friend has deserted you. You sit and drink and try to get euphoric, but all that happens is you feel depressed. But that doesn't mean you stop drinking. It's an addiction, and you have to do it."

An even worse effect of her drinking was that she spent much of her time in blackouts. Nan says that most people do not understand what blackouts really are.

"They are not simply a forgetting of certain events; rather it feels as if there is an electrical short circuit, that what is going on is simply not contained in the memory bank. It is like there is a little plug pulled in your head. Life to me for a couple of years was like coming into a movie in the middle. You find yourself in places or with people and have no knowledge of why you are there or who they are. They are talking to you in very familiar tones, so obviously you have some history together. That's where a lot of the lying associated with alcoholism comes in. You are asked where you were, a very logical question. But what can you say—I don't know? So you make something up. But then after a while you begin to accept these things as the way life is. And that's real bad when you start accepting it.

"Many times I would be in a total blackout state, and people would have no idea that there was anything strange about what I was doing. You tend to think of people in a blackout robbing banks or getting in car accidents and so forth. But they are doing perfectly normal things. The popular opinion is that a blackout is simply an alcoholic's excuse for what he was doing while he was drinking, but that's not true."

She adds sadly that there are several years that are almost entirely lost to her, of which she can remember only bits and pieces. She finds this very frustrating. But then she tosses up her hands, and in her own inimitable fashion says, "Maybe I'm better off not knowing!"

When I asked her what if anything in her background predisposed her to alcoholism, she replied:

"My parents were not drinkers. Drinking was not even discussed in my home. In later years I became aware that there were alcoholics on my father's side of the family, but this was never mentioned. I think my reading possibly contributed to the problem. I was a great reader, and there were lots of things I read in which drinking was glamorized: F. Scott Fitzgerald, Jack Kerouac, Allen Ginsberg, things I shouldn't have been reading.

"I was an overprotected child who was not allowed to go to the movies very much. My father did not permit any profanity used in my presence. In a restaurant if a party at an adjoining table spoke profanely, my father would go over to the table and tell them there were children there. I wasn't allowed to date unless it was strictly chaperoned.

"They were afraid of the wild streak in me. It was obvious from the beginning I was a wild child, and they were afraid for me. It was not that I didn't care when I hurt the people I loved. I was not a totally insensitive monster. I did have pangs of guilt and remorse when I did something to someone I loved. But it was not significant enough to produce any sort of behavior change.

"I had no idea alcohol was my problem. I thought I drank a little too much, but not enough to get into trouble. When I realized I was an alcoholic, it was a revelation, like a bolt out of heaven. You can't let yourself look at it; it's too important. If you look at it and say I am an alcoholic, then you have to do something about it.

"At Alcoholics Anonymous we're supposed to make reparation, but my father refused to see it, never wanted to discuss it. I thought at least I should pay him back some of his money, but he wouldn't talk about it. I did help him out later when he got Alzheimer's disease. It felt good to be a sober, functioning adult who was there when he needed me. But A.A. says to make direct amends; it doesn't say anything about the indirect kind. That would mean talking with him about wasting the money he lent me. But he wouldn't listen. I did the best I could."

When I asked Nan where she found the strength to overcome such a debilitating illness, she attributed her recovery to many things. First of all, she mentioned the A.A. program, to which she is eternally grateful. It is the touchstone of her life, and even after twenty years of sobriety, she attends meetings every day.

She swears by the Twelve Steps that are the foundation of the program. Most important to Nan was admitting that she was powerless over alcohol, accepting the notion that a higher power exists, and learning to look within herself instead of finding external excuses for her drinking.

But unlike many of its participants, she does not feel that A.A. alone can suffice, at least for her. In discussing her recovery, Nan said that one day twenty years ago, for reasons she does not understand, she "bottomed out." And suddenly she knew she could not go on in her present style of life. She then went for a twenty-eight-day program of treatment at Chit-Chat Farms, one of the oldest treatment centers for alcoholics, where she found a heavy concentration of A.A. principles. In addition she received both group and individual analysis, which she continued when she left the farm. She feels that the treatment was instrumental in setting her on the road to health.

Nan also gives her present husband, her third, credit for helping her overcome her addiction. A handsome, personable, youthful-looking man, he also is a recovered alcoholic. Apparently he does not feel he needs A.A. to stay well, and with the help of psychotherapy, he too has managed to stay sober for the twenty years he and Nan have been together.

When I asked if she thought she could have a relationship with an active alcoholic, she vigorously denied it. "Oh no," she stated categorically. "It is not possible to have a positive relationship with an active alcoholic. That person already has a primary relationship—with the bottle. You are always a poor second. But not all of my friends are in A.A.; I would say that about 50 percent of them are in the program."

A sponsor in A.A. is a recovered alcoholic who takes the responsibility of being available around the clock for new members, to listen to, guide, and to see the person through difficult times without resorting to alcohol. Most of all, Nan credits her husband's sponsor with contributing to her recovery. "Without him, I would not be sitting here talking to you today," she says poignantly. "He was that significant to me. He was a professional therapist, a warm, wonderful man, and he was there for me for over sixteen or seventeen years. He taught me how to live, how to care, how to feel. When he died a few years ago, I felt a part of me died with him." She is quiet as she wipes away a tear.

"Because of him, I have become the sponsor of two or three alcoholics. I know he cared about me. So I can only sponsor people I care about. If I do not like them, I will not sponsor them.

"I've also gone to individual therapists at other times of my life," she continues. "I had a few very bad years, in which my mother died and my father developed Alzheimer's disease. I had to confront my own unhealthy love and dependence on him. Any time I find myself in a situation A.A. is not equipped to handle, I return to therapy. Many people believe A.A. can give you all you need. I think it is a wonderful foundation and cornerstone of health, but it is not the total answer to all of life's problems. Some A.A. people are opposed to anything but A.A. But I feel much more mellow about it.

"I don't know why I recovered when I did," she continues thoughtfully. "Most of us did not choose to be alcoholics, nor did we choose to get well. The disease involves the whole person, spiritual, emotional, physical, and psychological. All of a sudden, the compulsion to drink just lifted for me." And, indeed, with all her insight, neither she nor I know precisely why she stopped drinking at the point she did. I doubt if anyone knows.

"It's so much better than it was when I was drinking," she continued. "I have a life. I love my home. I love this city. My husband and I went to school to learn our business, which I love. We work hard. It couldn't be more perfect. And I always work at the game plan. I consider it a miracle. I am very grateful."

"And have you any regrets?" I asked.

"No," she answered quickly. "I have a happy life. I'm sorry I put the people close to me through a lot of hell, but not for the experiences I've had. I'm grateful this has happened to me. Otherwise I would not be the person I am today."

The three women discussed in this chapter are different from each other in just about every way but the fact that all have successfully terminated an analysis. Each one, in a manner unique to her own personality, has invested newly freed energy in a rich, constructive, creative lifestyle.

Dream Interpretation:
A Refresher Course

After four years, Doris Field was leaving therapy; this was her last session. She looked at me with apprehension as she sat up on the couch, trying to find the courage to walk out the door forever.

"Are you sure I can keep on analyzing my own dreams?" she asked. "That I won't need you to help me? I've learned here how important dreams are."

"You've been analyzing your own dreams here for the past year," I assured her. "You've shown you can do it alone."

A mischievous smile took over her face as she said, "I just wanted to make sure."

"Write down the dream when you get up in the morning," I reminded her. "And then go through each element in it and associate to it with whatever comes into your mind, just as you did here. And, in particular, remember to explore whatever feelings are in the dream. They are an important clue to its hidden meaning."

I repeated Freud's statement, "An unanalyzed dream is like an unopened letter," and recommended she keep up with her emotional "mail."

She responded with fervor, "I know. Thoreau wrote, 'The unexamined life is not worth living.' I've learned here how true that is."

Doris left treatment and continued to analyze her own dreams. Years later, she is well and contented. She has not found it necessary to return to treatment.

One of the major reasons she is able to stay well is that she can analyze her own dreams. Dreams are the best single method for preserving our mental health. They are a unique product of the psyche. Artistic creation is sometimes said to be comparable, but in the opinion of the writer, it is not. Dreams are the only product of the mind not subject to manipulation. Dreams alone never lie.

Freud called dreams "the preserver of sleep." They satisfy our wishes and allow us to sleep undisturbed. They are meant to put to rest conflicts of the day, which have revived unsettled business from the past. When we awaken from a dream or a nightmare, that means the dream has failed in its major function as guardian of our sleep.

Dreams also allow feelings buried deep within to rise to the surface in harmless form. Like a caldron of fire searching to burst free, unconscious feelings can make trouble. When they erupt without our awareness, painful symptoms like compulsions and paranoia can result. When we accept that these feelings and wishes are ours, we can gain greater control over them. Then the terrifying monsters of childhood effervesce in the daylight.

Much energy is locked up in preventing thoughts and feelings from reaching consciousness. When one dares to look at the unconscious mind, it no longer is necessary to barricade the door to one's emotional basement. As a result, newfound powers are available, and energy is released for the important job of living.

Many who have finished their analysis have forgotten how to interpret their dreams. They need a refresher course. Some, who were in treatment with practitioners who were not particularly talented with dreams, need to develop new skills. Still others are happy and fulfilled enough to feel they do not require therapy, yet want to know more about the contents of their unconscious minds. Then there are people who, for whatever reasons, are afraid to go into therapy. Yet others are hardy souls who value their autonomy and won't place their lives in the hands of another. Another group cannot afford it, either in time or money. And some live far from a city where psychotherapists congregate. This chapter can prove a godsend for all of these would-be seekers of emotional health and freedom. It will be a how-to chapter for the analysis of dreams.

Dream interpretation is a skill, like any other. Knowledge and practice can teach this craft to those who sincerely wish to learn. If an individual is genuinely ill, of course he should consult a professional. But in my opinion there is no reason why a relatively normal person cannot learn to understand the productions of his mind. According to Ann Faraday, the renowned dream expert, a person who becomes deeply disturbed on looking within is not stirring up "monsters of the id."[1] Those monsters are just beneath the surface of the conscious mind, waiting to erupt under other circumstances at any moment.

The psychoanalysts have preempted the dream. I would like to return the dream to its original owners, the people.

As long ago as biblical times, wise men used their dreams to understand themselves and the world about them. The best example is the one of the seven lean and seven fat ears of corn.

It seems to me that Joseph was an intuitive farmer, wise enough in the interpretation of nature to understand its secrets, perhaps in ways he didn't even know consciously, so that he could accurately predict the good and the lean years. Because of his skill in the interpretation of dreams, many lives were saved from starvation.

Today a number of Indian tribes use dreams as part of their psychological life.[2] Foremost among this group are the Senoi Indians, a primitive Malaysian tribe of twelve thousand members whose way of life from government to health is dictated by dreams. From the time they are children, tribe members are taught how to use dreams to govern their personal life. It is interesting that anthropologists report that the Senoi have literally no incidence of emotional problems. Nor are there any terrifying dreams or nightmares, except during early childhood. This incredible record of mental health is ascribed to the tribe's commitment to self-awareness and self-control gained through their study of dreams. The dreamer is taught always to confront the enemy. He should never run away from dream images that frighten him, but stand and hold his ground, advance on the enemy, and attack. If the dream likenesses are too frightening, the dreamer is to call on dream friends and allies to help him conquer the enemy. The dreamer must always remember he has the power to gain victory for himself.

Another Senoi principle is to bring about a pleasant ending in a dream. Fears should always be faced and negative conditions made pleasant. If a Senoi dreams of being attacked by a friend, he goes to this friend in waking life and tells him about the dream. Some unintentional act of the friend may have offended the dreamer. Then the friend may give the dreamer a gift. Telling his friend the dream is an excellent technique of mental health and may well prevent the incident from happening again.

The tribe encourages that the gift be a creative one—a poem, a dance, a song, or a painting. The dreamer is encouraged on waking to actually carry out this gift giving. Thus the insights of the unconscious are carried over into waking life.

Every day tribe members, from children to old men and women, gather around the campfire to tell of their dreams, to try to grasp the meaning of hidden wishes, fears, and conflicts. Then members respond with helpful suggestions for handling the problem. For example, one adolescent boy spoke of being terrified in a dream by a lion from whom he barely escaped. Members of the tribe suggested he return to his dream that night and stand up to the lion. Because of this support, the boy dreamed again of the lion, but this time did not flee. The lion did not attack him but slowly stalked away. The adolescent gleefully told the tribe, "I wasn't afraid of him anymore." Then he added, "I think the lion was my father, the brave hunter, of whom I was always afraid." He had faced his fear about his strong-as-a-lion father and conquered it. What a wonderful way to resolve the Oedipus complex! Would that our society do as well!

As Jiminy Cricket so poignantly said to Pinocchio, "A dream is a wish your heart makes when you are fast asleep." The heart of a dream is usually a wish that has to be denied. The wish may be so simple as wanting to eat. If you are hungry and don't want to wake up, the dream is a way of eating your cake and keeping it too. Freud's daughter, Anna, was punished for a misdemeanor when she was only three years old. Her mother took delicious strawberries away from her. But in her dream that night, little Anna made her wish come true when she pictured herself eating "stwawberries."

The dream wish usually is a wish of childhood that has remained hidden for years because it was believed to be dirty or evil. As a rule it is tied to one or both of our strongest desires, our aggressive feelings in which we want to hurt or kill, or powerful sexual feelings that we felt as a child were taboo. Anna's dream, for example, may also allude to deeper wishes than eating "stwawberries."

Tom had a dream in late adolescence that he was walking by the ocean and saw two people lying together. He wondered, "Are they gay?" Shortly after, he became a practicing homosexual. His sexual orientation had not been acceptable to him before he had the dream because his father had taught him that gay men were sissies. In the dream it was two other people he wondered about, not himself. He had to experience the full power of his wish to love a man before he could allow himself the experience. The search for the underlying wish is always paramount to understanding the dream.

The most important tool for dream analysis is free association. To free associate you must allow every single thought, feeling, or sensation that floats through your mind and body to surface. When you are working alone, it helps very much to write these associations down as you go along. It is vital for this purpose that you do not allow embarrassment, guilt, fear, displeasure, depression, or the need to keep a good self-image keep you from your task.

If you are blocked and cannot continue, look at the content of what is stopping you. What are you feeling at this moment? If it is embarrassment, if you censor the idea by telling yourself it isn't important or your mother would say you are silly, don't let it keep you from your task. Do the same with painful anxiety; the danger you fear is probably from long ago. It may well have already happened. So continue anyway. Your persistence will pay off. The most wonderful insights can come after periods of resistance. Freud said that the greatest concentration of defenses are massed where the troops feel most threatened. So it is with the dream. We are most guarded at the point where the unconscious is closest to the surface. These mechanisms of defense can show us where we feel we need protection the most.

The first interpretation of a dream should deal with what Freud called the manifest content. By this he meant the dream as it actually was experienced. Are you grocery shopping in it? Visiting the dentist? Cleaning your house? Some task may well be clamoring to be finished. Note what action needs to be taken, and then listen to your dream and do it.

The next line to follow is that of the latent content, the underlying meaning of the dream as it is uncovered by analysis. In order to get to the latent content, free associate to each element in the dream in order to understand it. If you are associating correctly, thoughts that have never entered your mind should eventually result. If the dream has nothing new to say, then you haven't grasped its full meaning. Or at least you are not really finished. Free associate to it some more, either now or later.

Is your dream too long and complicated for you to understand? Can you not even fathom what it is about? Make up a title, as you would for a book. That frequently will help. One patient had such a dream, which left us both confused. I asked her to think of a title for it. She answered, "Rah-rah garbage!" And that's exactly what the dream was, a bunch of garbage meant to make the work of dream interpretation impossible. The dream took place at a time she was reliving memories of her crazy father. The dream confused me, as her father had confused her. It also expressed what she thought of the art of dream interpretation, as well as her "crazy" analyst! I hope the patient who had this dream is reading this book, for I understand her dream in retrospect much better than I did at the time. As the saying goes, "We grow too soon old and too late smart."

Another novel technique to unravel a deviously meandering dream is to give the plot in a sentence or two, as if it were a movie. I won't illustrate this method with a complete dream, because it wouldn't be worth the space it would take. But the simplicity of a single plot line has unraveled many a difficult dream. For example, a dream full of wanderings about a foreign city can seem to go on all night. Describing the frustrations encountered in every street will distract from the central theme. A brief description of the plot, such as, "I am a stranger in a strange land, who can't seem to find my way," presents a more astute psychological portrait of the dreamer.

Dreams can open up new options and set creative actions in motion. They can help reorganize the psyche and introduce us to new ways of coping. A good example is the case of Merton, the young man described in a previous chapter who came to analysis because he was flunking out of college. He was enrolled in a program to teach him his father's profession. He didn't like the program, and he didn't like his father. What better way to spite him than to flunk out of school? One day Merton dreamed he was on a glorious mountain. He found himself digging with pleasure deep down into the earth. When he woke up he said, "I'd really like to do that!" And shortly thereafter, he did. We'll never know whether Merton would have come to the same place in his life without having experienced the dream. But somehow, I doubt it very much.

Some people are afraid they can't cope on their own with material fresh from the unconscious. In my opinion this is an unnecessary fear. The hypnotist, regardless of his skill, is unable to make the individual in a trance do what he would resist when conscious. In both hypnosis and the dream state, our defenses are very strong and will only allow into consciousness what we are able to tolerate emotionally. Nevertheless, as indicated before, a person who feels overwhelmed by his dreams should seek consultation with a professional.

We originally repressed the material when we were small and were truly unable to cope with frightening or embarrassing feelings. Most people old enough to work with their dreams are stronger than they were as children and better able to handle material that once seemed overpowering. In the unconscious we all remain children. But when repressed material sees the light of day, the healthy adult can integrate what was insufferable to the child.

All dreams are attempted solutions of a conflict; a forbidden wish is expressed in a form that is acceptable to the conscience. For example, Rick cannot tolerate his own feelings of rage. He hates his wife because she browbeats him, but he cannot allow himself to know just how murderous he feels. To him, murderous feelings are a forbidden emotion. He is oblivious to the fact that feelings are different from actions. So he represses the wish and dreams she is hit by a car. After all, he didn't kill her in the dream. "It is not my fault," he rationalizes, "that she ran in front of the car." What he is not aware of is that he alone is the architect of his dream, and that it is he who has fancied her death. When he learned that wishes will not make it so, he was able to stand up to his wife's bullying in life and no longer found it necessary to kill her off in his dreams.

It is not enough to describe a dream or to think about it purely on an intellectual level. This might give insight, but it will not bring about change. For real growth to occur through dream interpretation, it is essential to seek out the feelings encoded in a dream. In the dream mentioned above, it was necessary for Rick to experience the full intensity of his hatred for his wife in order for the dream to be useful.

After forty years of analytic practice, I have discovered that by the end of a successful analysis, the story of a patient's life often can be summed up in one sentence. The theme of Clarissa's pathology was, "Mommy didn't love me, so I desperately wooed Daddy to have someone to love." With this understanding it became clear why she frantically sought lovers, yet rarely was happy with them. Similarly, when a person knows himself well, the theme of his life frequently can be headlined in a short dream. Mary dreamed, "As Barbara's brother was breaking her prized sofa, she wanted to strangle her mother." Mary understood immediately that it was she who wanted to strangle her mother, who openly preferred her brother. Mary's childhood had been tarnished by the oafish brother who was always permitted to take center stage and steal her place in the sun.

"A boat pulled out of the dock, and the undertow pulled her with it," was dreamed by Estelle during her treatment. She had been abandoned by her mother when she was a child, and she hadn't realized until she worked on this dream how much the loss had shattered her life.

Freud said that character is destiny. To the degree that character determines the outcome of life, dreams also can predict the future. The following dreams, by illustrating the character of the dreamers, predict their destiny.

John, the patient discussed in chapter 5, dreamed he had to drive down a narrow, lonely road to get home. There were obstacles every step of the way. Nevertheless, with superhuman strength he picked up the car and lifted it over the obstacles.

The narrow, rocky road stood for both his analysis and his life. Indeed, both were full of dangers, but this young superman found himself able to overcome them all. His resolution of the dream foretold a successful analysis and a successful life.

Millie's dream prophesied just the opposite. It gave me chills when I heard it. In it a little dog came up to her for affection and comfort. Millie pushed him away. In her treatment Millie, like the little dog, pushed away the warmth and comfort offered her by the therapist. Shortly after having this dream, Millie left treatment. Years after, I heard she had killed herself. The dream indeed was a prediction of her failure to take what life had to offer, leaving her an empty existence with no alternative but death.

I myself have had a number of prediction dreams dealing with changes in career. When I first began analytic training at the National Psychological Association for Psychoanalysis, I dreamed that a circle of my male teachers (they all were male at the time) had picked me up by the shoulders, making me as tall as they. Thus they made me bigger than I would have been, as psychoanalysis indeed has made me a bigger person than I was. The entire group was bathed in a white light, almost as if we were surrounded by a halo. I think even back then I unconsciously knew I would have a highly successful career as an analyst.

Forty years later I had another "halo" dream. I had just made the decision to leave my analytic practice and work full-time at writing. In this dream another group of people, perhaps family and friends, threw a little bird up into the air, where it flew to a similar group of people who safely caught it. Then the bird grew more confident of its powers and flew off into the distance alone. This was followed by a second dream in which my computer chair glowed with a soft fuchsia light. Perhaps the dream is saying that my second career will be as successful as the first.

I recently had another dream I believe contains a prediction. I have a beautiful fire opal that my husband gave to me. Someone really admired it yesterday—the trigger that set off the dream. In the dream the opal has grown much larger than it is and sparkles in the sunlight. The gold that encloses the opal has more than doubled in size and weight (and, incidentally, in value). The dream suggests that memories of my husband are bright indeed and will increasingly light up my life.

I find this an amusing, if hopeful, interpretation. Several widowed women, including my sister, have told me that the longer their husbands are dead, in their minds, the better they look. I wouldn't be surprised if this development holds true for me as well.

Every now and then in a lifetime there occurs what I call the "landmark dream." These are milestones that mark our passage through life and indicate the beginning of a new era. My dream about the rosy computer chair was just such a turning point, ushering in the end of one phase and the beginning of a new one.

Art had such a landmark dream. After the dream, he felt loved and treasured for the first time in his memory. His mother had died when he was a little child. He remembered very little about her, with no feelings at all of her loving presence. One day after several years of analysis, Art dreamed of his mother's garden. It was lush and green, and overrun with flowers of many kinds. As he described each of the flowers, I felt an uncanny sensation. It was as though the garden grew increasingly alive in our presence. The fragrance of the flowers was overpowering, and I could sense the feel of the cool morning dew on the grass.

Then Art started to sob, "I remember . . . I remember . . . the way she tenderly knelt on the dirt, the marvelous armfuls of flowers that filled every room in the house. The way she loved and tended her flowers . . . that's how she tended me. Always a gentle touch, always a fragrant smell, always patiently standing by waiting for me to grow. Yes, I really had a mother. I've found her here in this room."

How can you tell a landmark dream from any other? Many times you can't. It is one of those phenomena easier to recognize after the fact than at the time of its occurrence. Although I was aware it was a very important dream when he reported it, only in looking back can I see how much of a landmark it was. For the felt knowledge that his mother loved him changed Art's life thereafter. Since then I have found that certain characteristics tend to suggest that these dreams are highly significant. Like the two examples given, mine and Art's, they often are in color, indicating that the dream content is just coming into awareness. When not in color, they may be rife with other senses, such as in Art's dream. Perhaps the kinesthetic sense is uppermost, so that bodily feelings are strongly present. This sensual intensity suggests that sooner or later the latent dream content, if not already conscious, will appear in future dreams.

Repetitive dreams are particularly important. They indicate that something once happened to us that was too overwhelming or frightening to be integrated all at once. This kind of dream is a means of getting a handle on the experience or getting on top of it. One man was attacked by a lion, who caught him and actually began chewing on his arm. The man was rescued before he was killed, but every night for thirty years after, he dreamed he was attacked by the lion. In this way, little by little, he was trying to master the horror of the experience.

In looking over this dream, it occurred to me how similar it is to the dream of the Senoi adolescent. And yet, if you compare the dreams, you see they have entirely different meanings. Symbols can be useful to a certain extent, but its deeper meaning can be grasped only through the associations of the dreamer.

Every aspect of a dream somehow refers to the dreamer. In the dream mentioned above in which Rick's wife ran in front of a car, Rick was able to deny that he wished to kill her by making the driver of the car the murderer. By having Rick understand that *he* is the driver, in disguise, he was able to experience the full intensity of his hatred for his wife.

An event of the previous day is always the trigger that sets off a dream. A specific incident or feeling brings to mind a buried scene of the past that is still unresolved and disturbing. One way to get to its meaning is to go through the events of the day. One woman had a dream in which she wanted to lash out at her father because he had refused to allow her to wear a sexy black dress she had just bought for a high-school dance. In her analytic session she recalled the day her father had ordered her to take off the dress, at which point she burst into tears, fled to her bedroom, and told herself angrily, "Someday I'll get even with him."

What had set off the dream? She remembered that the day before, she had stood in front of the window at Bergdorf Goodman's, staring at a sleek black-velvet dress, wishing she could buy it. At that moment she did not associate it to the sexy black dress she once owned. But during her session the next day, in which she described her dream, she suddenly said in surprise, "Yesterday I saw a lovely black dress just like the one my father made me take off years ago. It was in the window at Bergdorf's, and I stood looking at it wistfully."

The dress in the window had reawakened her earlier experience with her father and her rage at his order not to wear it. A rage she had buried twenty years before had surged to the surface of her mind as she lay asleep. During her session she allowed her anger to emerge. "What a mean man!" she exclaimed. "I'll never forgive him for ruining what could have been the most exciting night of my high-school years."

A most practical use of dreams is suggested by Father Charles Thomas Cayce.[3] According to him, if you consistently record your dreams, "you will find answers to problems from everyday life popping up in the dream state—how to deal with a situation at work, handle specific relationships, etc."

I myself have had this experience. Once I misplaced some valuable papers and was looking for them quite frantically. Before going to sleep one night, I sternly ordered myself, "Now you go to sleep and dream about where you put the papers!"

To my great surprise, I did just that. In my dream I clearly saw the papers at the bottom of a cluttered drawer in my desk. On awakening, I wasn't very hopeful, as I had already searched that desk with what I considered thoroughness. Nevertheless, I went through it again. And sure enough, there were the papers at the bottom of the desk drawer, just as my dream had pictured!

Patients have asked, "How do you get to remember a dream? They often are so fleeting I cannot get hold of them." I tell them how I work with my own dreams. If I wake up with a dream, I don't leap out of bed to get on with the day. Instead I lie there for a few moments with my eyes closed and go over all the details of the dream in my head until it is set. I may associate to it or not, depending on my state of mind. Then I move to my computer and write it down. A dream is an ephemeral work of creativity, and like most creations, must be recorded immediately, or it will evaporate. My mother once wisely told me, "If you have a dream, don't look out the window, or you'll forget it." She meant that if I looked out on the outer world, I would lose touch with the inner world of my dream.

After writing down the dream on the computer, if the meaning has not yet become clear, I might make a copy for myself to carry around. Then, at odd moments of the day, while waiting for a patient, perhaps, or riding on a bus, I will take out the dream and muse on each element of it. First I will look for the literal meaning, to finish up the events of the previous day. Then I associate to each element. This process will continue until I feel I understand the dream. Then I put it away, to take out at a later date when I have another dream that deals with a similar theme. I do this because there is infinitely greater understanding of a dream seen in the context of a dream series than when it stands on its own.

If you have ever read all the works of one novelist, you know the difference in depth of understanding of the author between reading one book and the whole series. So it is with dreams. When you have a progression of them, you will get insight you cannot possibly get from only one. When I wrote the book *Who Killed Virginia Woolf?*, I read everything she had written, including forty books, six diaries, and six books of letters. Through this extensive reading of one writer, I obtained a far deeper understanding of her works and her life than I possibly could have gathered from the study of one book. Similarly, you can reach a much deeper meaning of a dream by seeing it within the framework of a series. This is scientifically demonstrated in *Dream Portrait,* in which my colleagues and I analyze nineteen sequential dreams of a former patient of mine.

As I stated earlier, I have recorded some of my dreams since I was twenty-one years old. I couldn't bring most of them to analysis at the time, as I hadn't yet begun it. Looking back recently on my early dreams, I had a shocking revelation. My younger brother had died from cerebral meningitis at the age of eighteen. I thought I had survived his death relatively intact. But in rereading the dreams, I see that I had very nearly cracked up. As I indicated before, one of the symbols I used was that of a "crazy woman" who wanted to kill me with a knife. It is easy to recognize now, although not at the time, who the "crazy woman" was.

Another dream I had around that time led to further, if belated, insight. I dreamed there was a huge stone in the depths of the sea. But when I recorded the dream, I wrote *debts* instead of *depths*. This "slip of the pen" brought to awareness the burden of my hidden guilt.

Understanding our dreams delivers us from the weight of a massive psychic load. It allows us to face haunting memories, like the death of my brother, and to deal with them as adults. So long as such agony remains buried, it will fester within like pus in a boil. Making it conscious is akin to lancing the boil. Feeling the "depth" of my guilt about the death of my brother enabled me to overcome the unconscious conviction that I had been responsible for it.

This dream highlights another principle of dream interpretation. According to Freud, every word uttered about the dream should be treated as part of the dream. Writing *debt* instead of *depth* wasn't simply a slip of the pen, but illuminated the meaning of the dream. Similarly, a remark such as, "This dream is too short," could well refer to an element in the dream. I'll leave it to your imagination to guess what that "element" might frequently be.

Details of a dream are especially important. Where does the dream take place? Sometimes the locale will indicate a scene from the past that illustrates the event of the day. A patient, Murray, dreamed he was sleeping with me. When asked where the dream took place, he said, "In my mother's bedroom!" The dream illustrated that this little Oedipus felt about the analyst now as he did about his mother when he was very small.

Who are the people in the dream? Are they men, women, or children? Young, old, blond, or brunette; tall, short, fat, or thin? Invariably these details will give the interpreter a clue as to who the antagonists are in present-day life and/or who the originals were in the childhood of the dreamer. One patient dreamed of a woman who wore large round glasses, who didn't look like anyone she knew. When asked who wore such glasses, she responded, "My grandmother, of course!" And then we understood the dream. These particulars are abounding in memories that lead to unveiling the deeper meanings of the dream.

Freud told us that "every dream stands on two legs." By this he meant that every dream has two meanings, one concerning a present-day conflict and the other a similar situation rooted in the past. In the "little Oedipus" dream, Murray had sexual feelings for the analyst, but felt they were "bad" and repressed them. His association to his mother's bedroom tells us that Murray, like every little boy, had similar desires for his mother that he felt made him a bad boy. To keep away these unacceptable feelings, he squelched all of his erotic desires. As a result, he had no active sex life at all.

The "other leg" of Murray's dream dealt with his feelings for the analyst. After he could face the erotic feelings for me that he originally had felt for his mother, he was able to find a wonderful sex partner who later became his wife.

No two dreams are the same and no two dreamers alike. Our individuality is always present in a dream. Our genes, the amount of sexual and aggressive energy we are born with, our childhood, our fate, as well as the circumstances of everyday life, all of these contribute to make each of us a unique individual, and each dream a reflection of that singularity. That is why a dream cannot adequately be interpreted without the associations of the dreamer. Without them, no matter how brilliant the interpretation, each attempt is just an intellectual exercise. Nevertheless, Freud told us that there are a few universal symbols, to which the analyst can resort for guidelines when the meaning of the dream is obscure. Foremost among these are the sexual symbols, in other words, an umbrella or a house standing for the female genitals and a tower or sharp pointed object, the penis.

Sometimes the meaning of a dream remains obscure even when associations seem fairly complete. Then a tactic that often works is one used by the Gestalt psychologists. Because they believe that every aspect of a dream refers to the dreamer, they have the dreamer act out each part of his dream. This is done by saying, "I am a . . ." for each dream element. For example, I had the following dream shortly after I moved to Key West:

"I am on a highway on my way to an airport. Off to the right is a huge structure of very light pink. It is somewhat square, with rounded edges, something like a giant beehive or a cliff dweller's many-celled residence. There are various lines or roads of many different levels in it that people live on. (The different passages remind me of the GUM department store in Moscow, which I visited a few years ago).

"I am on the highway." I think, I *am* on the high way, in my new career.

"I am on the way to the airport." Well, I always am, including the trip to Russia. At the airport, I will "fly high," symbolically as well as literally.

"I am a complex structure of many levels. I am busy as a beehive." Recently I was thinking of how many different types of writing I have done, professional articles, psychobiography, humor, poetry, short stories, historical fiction, a novel, and now this book. I certainly write on many levels. Perhaps my personality is multilayered, as well.

"My various levels are connected, as in GUM's department store, where there are many bridges between various sections and tiers." I hope so. After many years of analysis, I would like to believe that my conscious and unconscious minds have easy access to each other.

"I am somewhat square with rounded edges." Well, I *am* "somewhat square," in the sense of looking conventional. When I was a young woman, people I didn't know guessed I was a secretary, in later years, perhaps a teacher, if not a housefrau. Rarely have I been taken for a specialist in psychology or a writer. But my edges are "rounded"; I have taken the edge off the squareness by being myself.

"The interesting part of my structure is what is inside." Yes, I think that is correct.

"It is odd that my structure exists at all. There is no other edifice of its kind." That also is true of me, at least in regard to my family. I have always been different from the others. They were puzzled by the strange child who was always sitting with her nose buried in a book. There was even a story that I was left on the doorstep by a gypsy. I am an anomaly in a family of housewives and businessmen.

"I am light pink in color." Red is my favorite color—vibrant, passionate, and strong. But I am not a "red" person, although I would like to be. Pink is a subtle, quieter shade of red. That is more how I see myself, with some of the attributes of redness, but muted in later years. Incidentally, the color predicts that there will be more of this "structure" in the future.

"I am a beehive, swarming with action. Within me dwells many a "bee" (be); there is the queen bee, many worker bees, and even, I fear, some drones." Yes, there are many levels of be(e)ing, for me as well as the bees.

"I am a department store," in that I sell my services, both therapeutic and literary, the latter of many kinds.

"I am a bridge between many levels." I am a narrow link between the past and the future, a connection for my children between my parents and my grandchildren.

If we are to follow this line of dream interpretation, I can say, "Although it may not seem that way on superficial acquaintance, I am an unusual person, one of a kind, with a subtle somewhat-muted personality. I have many different aspects to my nature; some are regal, some hardworking, and others indolent. These different selves are not sealed off from one another but always remain connected. I myself am the link between present and past generations. I already have a 'high way' of life and am moving toward another direction, in which I will soar to the skies."

I recently appeared on a series of radio programs, as part of a book tour, to publicize *Who Killed Virginia Woolf?* One show, on station WFAS, was on dreams. Listeners were asked to call in with dreams they wished to have interpreted on the air. The program was extremely well received; in fact the station broadcast it a second time, as the most popular show of the week.

Long after the show was over, listeners called in asking to have their dreams analyzed. One woman was so insistent, in my absence, that she pleaded with the station secretary to analyze her dream. This reaction of a relatively unsophisticated audience indicates that the public wants to learn more about its dreams. Despite the need for caution in interpreting to unknown dreamers with no follow-up support, I was surprised to find that there was not a single dream about which I could not make some enlightening remark acceptable to the dreamer.

The following dreams are some of those called in by listeners, along with the interpretations given to them.

Marty phoned in, "I've been in a good relationship with a lady for about five years, and I dreamed she was in bed with another man. I was befuddled by it— we've not had any major problems or anything.

"The dream reminds me that when I was in the air force, I got a 'Dear John' letter from a girl I was going to marry. I got her a ring and everything. She had written me every day for fifteen months. Then two weeks before I came home, her mother sent me a letter and told me her daughter had gotten pregnant and had to elope and get married."

I suggested to Marty that the betrayal of his first girlfriend was so terrible that he hasn't gotten over it yet. He is terrified it will happen again. By reenacting the scene with his present love in the dream, he is trying to overcome the incident that was too overwhelming to master at the time. Marty felt relieved by my comments and happy that I felt the dream had little to do with his present girlfriend. Needless to say, I did not tell him that he had yet to get over the betrayal of his first love, his mother.

The price we pay for keeping our head in the sand is sometimes too expensive. Take this dream of Laurie's:

"I have a dream that I keep having over and over again. I live in this house that's standing on stilts on the beach. It's very rickety. The waves keep hitting it, and I'm scared it will fall down and drop into the ocean."

The dream tells us that Laurie is having a hard time in her life, that things are very rickety for her, indeed, an interpretation she instantly agreed with. But she doesn't really want to know about it, or she wouldn't have to dream it. A dream really is a metaphor. The shaky house stands for how she feels in her unconscious. It would be better for her to be aware of her feelings in order to learn how to cope with them.

Elizabeth was in her early twenties during World War II. She had a dream recently that the Japanese were invading the country.

"I'm really steamed up over Japanese imports," she said. "The dream was very vivid, and I woke up in a cold sweat. The Japanese are taking over my country; they bought Rockefeller Plaza, marinas, Firestone, and Paramount Studios, among others."

I replied, "Your waking up 'in a cold sweat' tells us that you *really* are scared that the Japanese are taking over the country, just as you must have been terrified during World War II."

Then thinking perhaps that fear of the Japanese probably wasn't strong enough to set off such a terrifying dream, I asked her, "Is there someone in your current life trying to invade your privacy?" Taken by surprise, she agreed, and told me about her current lover who wanted to move in with her. I said, "It is better to learn to say no than to allow yourself to be taken advantage of."

Sharon has a recurring dream early every morning. She dreams: "I'm lost; then I wander and I struggle and never find what I am struggling about or the exit I'm looking for. It's so bad that I have a headache every morning when I wake up."

Sharon acknowledged that she really feels lost in life and doesn't know who she is. She needs to find out more about herself and what she really wants. Sharon would do well to seek psychotherapy to help her in her quest to find herself.

Marie dreams that she can fly. "You take a small bounce, and you end up between thirty or forty feet off the ground, and you just soar around block after block after block. You glide around a little longer, and then you just gradually come down. It's a delightful dream. I wake up very happy."

Marie is lucky, if she restricts her escape to her dreams. She has found a pleasant way to take a little vacation when things get rough. She knows how to get "above it all."

The dream is also one of disguised orgasm, but I didn't give Marie that interpretation!

Eleanor dreamed that her grandchild got hurt. Shortly after, her son divorced his wife. Eleanor asked, "Do you think the dream was an omen that something bad was going to happen?"

"No," I answered, "I don't think it was an omen. But I believe you are a very perceptive woman who unconsciously picked up on the troubled vibes of your son."

Some people deny their fears, only to have them sneak out in their dreams. Bill had this dream shortly before he had surgery:

"I don't think I was worried about the operation at all. I was looking out the window onto a roadway, and I saw this dark casket with a spray of flowers on it. I could see the different colors of the flowers on top of the casket. Do you think I could have been worrying about the operation?"

Here I faced a dilemma. Would it be dangerous to take away his defenses? Should I allow him to go on fooling himself? I decided to take a chance and tell him the truth, because the very fact that he was reporting the dream to me suggested he was ready to hear its meaning.

"Yes," I told him, "I think you are 'worrying' about the operation and are too frightened to let yourself know it." Bill gratefully agreed. His worst fear was that he would die. Now that he knows about his terror, perhaps he will allow his doctor or minister to reassure him.

On a radio show you cannot go into much depth about a dream. But in a day-to-day relationship with yourself, there is great satisfaction to be derived if you can follow through on the contents of a dream and slowly relate it to threatening memories.

How do the dreams of an analyzed person differ from those of other people? Ella Freeman Sharpe presents an erudite portrait of the similarities and differences.[4] According to her, the concept of the analyzed person chiefly conveys the capacity to go about life independently and effectively. The individual is able to experience pleasure, accompanied by zest and a feeling of well-being.

She states that the analyzed person will continue to dream, for analysis does not analyze away the unconscious, and instinctual and infantile wishes always will remain. But while infantile conflict is indestructible, the demand for satisfaction of the wish has been relinquished. To take a blatant example, John, the "Little Oedipus," knew he wanted to sleep with his mother, but unlike the time when he was three years old, he never expected to do it.

Analyzed or unanalyzed though the individual may be, the function of the dream is always to preserve one's sleep through the conversion of a disturbance into gratified infantile wishes.

To return to the original question, then, How do the dreams of the analyzed person differ from those of the unanalyzed?

For one thing, the wishes are less disguised. What formerly was met with horror now can be seen as the wish of a child. John became able to accept that he wanted to make love to his mother. But his affect became quite different. Instead of feeling guilt or shame he could enjoy the fantasy. Thus we can say, along with Ella Freeman Sharpe, that the superego is modified to permit instinctual gratification and to accept the universality of infantile wishes. She also reports that after analysis, dreams tend to be much shorter and that analyzed people rarely will have anxiety dreams, nightmares seldom if ever. Nor will wild animals represent the animal nature of the dreamer. Analyzed people will not experience the repetitive dream, Sharpe continues. The long, complicated dream is rare, as is the dream that is very beautiful. The reason for this is that analysis has made possible the satisfaction of instinct and/or its sublimation. It does not have to be gratified through a dream.

In my experience all children have fantasies about their parents and themselves that make things seem more frightening than they actually are. By bringing these fantasies to the light of day, we relieve the pressure of emotions disavowed because we thought them dangerous to our well-being. That may have helped us survive as children. But for healthy adults the repression is more dangerous than the fantasy itself.

Facing these buried feelings and wishes becomes far easier once we find the courage to explore our inner selves. As we grow to accept our secret nature as it appears in dreams, allow our feelings to be expressed freely, and distinguish the "real" from the "unreal," we will find a sense of ease and maturity that leads to a richer, more fulfilling life.

10

Live Out
Your Unlived Dreams

Sometimes people who have terminated analysis successfully still find themselves dissatisfied. Freud spoke of the cured neurotic as one who then is subjected to "ordinary everyday unhappiness." Can this "ordinary everyday unhappiness" be "cured" along with the neurosis? I think it often can.

Few people are fortunate enough to live out every important aspect of their personalities, to experience all the inherent possibilities of their being. Sometimes these unlived aspects of the self clamor to be heard. The less they are listened to, the more blaring the psychological tumult. Tuning them out is a major reason for depression, particularly at certain periods of life like mid-life and old age. Those are the times it is normal to ask, "Is this all there is? Am I never to have any more? Won't my wishes ever come true?" When the answer seems to be no, depression is often the result.

These phases sometimes are accompanied by desperation, as the last possibility of realizing our dreams slowly slips away. Then one must ask certain questions of oneself, such as, "Will

211

I never have the love affair I dream of? Will I never be the great artist of my dreams? Won't I ever learn French? Play the guitar? Or lose that extra ten pounds I've lugged about for decades? Can't I ever move out of this town and live in my cherished city? Or leave the city and inhabit the beautiful countryside? How about traveling to Timbuktu? Must I die without ever having been there? Won't I ever get to take that trip around the world? Have red hair? Learn to tap dance? Pilot a plane? Visit the Seven Wonders of the World? How can I die without ever having seen the Parthenon? Be like Shirley Valentine, the heroine of the play of that name, and book your passage to Greece. Whatever your dream is, "book" it now, before it is too late.

What is *your* unlived fantasy, the dream you have never been able to fulfill? Has it been lost in your effort to conform? Probably, like most people, you've tried to be a good boy or girl all your life. You work hard at your job, are a conscientious mate, raise your children the best you can, and are even responsible for your aging parents. Suddenly you are shocked to realize that the years have marched on inexorably without your being aware of it. You could always tell yourself, "Next year is the year I'll do my X." Now the number of remaining years have shrunk; who knows how many (or how few) are left? Now you conclude with alarm, "There may never be any X!"

Now is the moment the healthy personality awakens and protests, "What about me? When is my turn? I'd better do it now, before it is too late." This is the time a constructive crisis can begin. For it is the only "now" we ever will have to fill in the missing blanks.

What is your unlived fantasy? Study it well and see if there isn't a way to make it come true. Dreams do not always have to remain dreams. Keeping them purely in the realm of fantasy may be the path to depression and despair. Perhaps they are more possible to gratify than you think. If not, can you possibly compromise, to own even a small piece of the pie? You are a forty-year-old woman, and you've always wanted to be a ballet dancer. Well, for that it is a bit late. But you can always take ballet lessons. Greta Garbo had a bar built into her apartment and practiced every day of her life. Meet your unlived self and bring it out of the closet. Tom Clancy was an insurance salesman before he wrote *The Hunt for Red October*, the first of many of his novels to reach the best-seller list. Anaïs Nin dreamed she lived on a houseboat in Paris. She promptly moved into one on the Seine and found a fulfilling and exciting life. How many of her books would have been written if she hadn't followed her dreams?

What are your unsatisfied longings? Tell them to yourself in the stillness of the night, and see if you can at least partially satisfy them. Have you always wanted to try interior design? Go back to school and get your credentials. "But I will be fifty years old when I'm finished!" you wail. "How old will you be then if you are *not* a designer?" I ask. As Goethe said, "Whatever you can do or dream you can, begin it."

A more modern example of living out your unlived dreams is found in W. P. Kinsella's famous award-winning novel, *Shoeless Joe*, which became the hit movie, *Field of Dreams*, starring Kevin Costner. In the story, the Costner character heard a voice in a hallucination that said to him, "If you build it, they will come." It turned out that he had a deep-seated wish to build a baseball diamond far away from any city, where ball teams are usually located. Against all logic and common sense, he built the diamond on his farm, and of course it became a great success. I suspect Kinsella, too, lives by the philosophy of his hero, which may well account for his ability to write the book and his tremendous success as a writer.

Jessica is a good example of a healthy approach to a "neurosis." She had a fairly nice figure, certainly a respectable one.

At five feet four inches, she weighed perhaps 120 pounds. But the women she admired most were elegant society ladies. You know the type, the lunchers at chic restaurants who can "never be too rich or too thin." Like them, Jessica yearned to be a "social x-ray." Friends thought she looked just fine and pooh-poohed her secret desire. As her analyst, I would have preferred to analyze her "neurosis" and have her go on to another goal. But analysis or not, Jessica was determined to make her wish come true.

In her fifties, she visited a spa that dictated a rigid diet and vigorous exercise program. To everyone's surprise, the spartan regime worked. Jessica lost a lot of weight and achieved the image she had always wanted. She was right; on her it looked good! For the first time in her life, she was beautiful. The look was exactly right for her and brought out her hidden inner self. With surprise, I realized that it was not a vain, cosmetic change she had sought, but an essential part of her being, for Jessica had brought together her inner and outer selves, which enabled her to alter the setting of her life. Her action confirmed my conviction that no one else can tell you what to do, that whatever the credentials of the "advisor," it is only our inner voices that always speak the truth.

Jessica kept up the health program after she left, until it became a way of life. She had known what would suit her best and had found the strength to achieve it. She still weighs ninety-eight pounds and is a happy and healthy woman. And now that she has achieved her "look," she no longer is concerned with her weight.

Katie had always wanted to be an artist but felt forced to spend her youth earning her living as a teacher. In her forties she became depressed. Feeling it was now or never, she gathered up her courage and took a leave of absence. Then, for reasons she didn't understand, she felt pulled to go to Santa Fe to paint.

There she discovered a unique method of capturing the colors of the desert, which gave her satisfaction as well as adulation. With a leap of faith at the end of her leave, she moved to New Mexico. There she became a well-known regional painter, who earns her living doing the work she loves. Incidentally, she hasn't been depressed since she moved to Santa Fe.

Bryce's story has a similar ending, with a different twist. A highly successful accountant, he became bored with the work. He felt it was no longer a challenge, that he needed work involving greater emotional depth. Against all advice of professionals, as well as of friends and family, he entered an analytic training program. He interested his wife in applying as well. They turned out to be gifted analysts and established rewarding social lives with their new colleagues. An unforeseen bonus of their change in career was that their new profession brought them closer together. The two are now happily engaged in the full-time practice of psychoanalysis.

Rosa was a woman in her forties who had desperately wanted to get married all her adult life. For one reason or another, her liaisons had never worked out. She was left with a desperate hunger for children and a despair that she would never have them. After much soul-searching, she decided to adopt a child. She tried for a number of years but was unable to succeed. To her despair she discovered that agencies didn't want to give children to single women. Then, attempts to subsidize a pregnant woman in order to adopt the child also failed. I admired the persistence of this brave woman who refused to admit defeat. After researching conditions for adoption all over the world, she took a trip to Korea. There she finally was able to re-solve her quest and returned with two lovely little girls. Now, as a single mother, she is happily raising her children. Perhaps it was the decision of choice for Rosa, after all. For she said that once she found her children, she no longer wanted a man.

Colleen O'Leary is a young woman who came into analysis in her middle thirties for relationship problems and left to follow her own inner dream. She wanted to give up a wonderful career, family, and friends to seek a new life in Ireland, where she could rediscover her roots. She went to Ireland, and as a result is a most happy woman today. I have been corresponding with her now and then since she moved and asked if she would like to be included in this book.

She answered that she was not sure of what I had in mind in terms of length or detail but would be delighted to be in the book, whatever the requirements. She then described her life before and after analysis in the following manner:

My analysis with Alma Bond lasted about three years, until I left New York for Dublin, Ireland, where I now live.

I presume that had I not left the United States, I would have continued the analysis, perhaps for another year or two. But in that realization is one of the key attributes of the analytic experience: that I *could* leave, could judge what I needed, and could expect that Alma as therapist would support me in leaving her, therapy, and my life as it had been in New York.

My assumption about therapy was that it often engendered long-term attachment to the therapist. But more fundamentally, my family background was one of the tremendous burden and responsibility of supporting fragile parents and of being unable to separate from a primitive, narcissistic mother.

My experience of leaving therapy and moving abroad—huge steps in achieving separation—was of complete support for me, my needs and desires. I vividly remember my amazement at not being scoffed at, criticized, or held back by my analyst. My move at the time was not the most "responsible" one: My partner, child, and I got off a secure career track and took a bold step away. But given awareness and support in the therapy, I found the strength to be true to myself.

My original family and I had emigrated from Ireland when I was a child, to lead a rocky, unhappy existence in America. But my bonds to Ireland lay very deep, and clearly I needed to redo or undo the emigration and return on my own terms.

That support in leaving, in deciding *for my needs, not hers*, is a strong aspect of the therapy. Another is the experience of Alma, as therapist, as the "good mother," who understood the person I am, supported me, and had confidence in me, including talking quite directly to me. I was able to tell her more, because of the lack of judgmentalism, for with her I experienced criticism, good or bad, as being *in my interest*.

That sense, in and of itself, was profoundly important and helpful.

A most significant aspect of the therapy was related to my father, a distant man who died of alcoholism. Much of my memory and feelings for him were very blocked, and overcome by the "noise" of a hugely demanding mother. But I always had a latent identification with him, and the therapy and my feelings, to my surprise, focused on him. There were some horrible, painful dreams, which led up to my finally feeling the pain of his death and his absence in my life.

I come, then, to the "gift" of the therapy, the legacy. When I entered therapy, I was two years into a relationship with someone I profoundly loved and the child we raise together. I was extremely insecure and anxious that the relationship would not last, I would be left, and the dream would fade—perhaps a self-fulfilling prophecy.

But in the therapy with Alma, I was "guided" (directed!) away from my absorbing and self-defeating anxieties to looking at, feeling, and reliving the early experiences with my parents and my identifications with them. All of these were programmed, if I had not had help, to reliving their own histories of ending up alone.

And I resisted, steadily, surely, the root and branch approach to taking apart the fundamental causes of my anxiety and fear of abandonment.

And so, I am now ten years into the relationship of my life, and *not* alone and bewildered as to it all. I am infinitely more secure, happily in love with a beautiful partner and our child.

Oh, I still have problems. I worry about losing all that I have, this wonderful place I've somehow come to.

But the fact is, the reality is, I'm here, I got "here" to good love and a good life far away from where I was, in the country of my dreams.

I love you, Alma—and I'll always thank you.

Joan Eldredge is a former Gestalt therapist whose life is dedicated to the art of living according to her inner needs. For fourteen years, on and off, her home has been a recreational vehicle. She spends most of the winter near Key West, where she parks her van by the ocean. Then, sometime in May she usually takes off for destinations unknown.

"Where are you going next?" I asked her in March. "I don't know yet," she answered.

"How did this way of life begin for you?"

"After I was divorced, I was terrified to be alone. I decided there was no reason to be afraid, and I was going to get over it. So I bought my van and a little tent and drove out to the mountains. I slept in terror that first night, all alone in my little tent, with the flaps open and the wind blowing through. There is no way to lock a tent! But nothing awful happened. I got over my anxiety, and now I go anywhere I want alone."

"Tell me about last year."

"That was partially decided for me," she answered. "I had two new grandchildren, one on each coast. So I spent most of the year traveling between the two. I spent most of my time in New Mexico and Arizona.

"Have you ever spent any time in the desert? It is indescribably lovely. I was in Arizona and saw a sign saying Desert

Museum. I started to go there, and then I thought, 'Am I crazy?' Here I am in this magnificent desert and rushing off to see a desert museum. I'll go to the museum tomorrow. Then I took out my beach chair and sat out in the sands. Did you ever watch the patterns in the sand in the desert? I sat there for hours, looking at the way the wind forms ever-new designs. Then I watched the birds hopping in the sand."

The pièce de résistance of Joan's lifestyle came when she met a man who became very special to her. She said that a friend introduced them late one night in a parking lot. There was no light, and she could hardly see him, could barely make out his size and shape, let alone his face. Nevertheless, a little voice in her said, "This man is the one." They lived together happily for four years.

"I was still married when I was going through my analysis, and I had gone back to school to get my second master's degree. My analysis gave me a clearer picture of the interactions within my family—my growing-up family, that is, and I could see more patterns that were there when looking at it through the analytic eye. But I found that when I came on some hard times, my analyst said to come back when I was feeling better. I was forced to work it out alone. So there were periods when I was changed by life circumstances, as well as therapy.

"When I was a child, my father took us on many trips all over the country. I had a wonderful time with him. He would teach me to stop and look at the land. One time we went by a dune, and he said to my brother and me, wouldn't it be fun to roll down it? So we did. The trips when I was a child traveling cross country left an imprint, so that after my divorce it didn't seem like a far-out idea to take off and go cross-country again.

"I always told my patients when they were going through a crisis to try to keep some sort of stability in their lives to hold the framework together so that everything wasn't dissolving around them during the crisis, and that they would have support from familiar people, job, and so forth. But in my own case, I didn't do that after my divorce. This little voice inside me said, 'Take off to the land.' I wasn't sure whether it was a feeling of being pushed or pulled by the 'instruction.' Really, when it came right down to it, it didn't matter. This was what I needed to do, to leave the community, and go off by myself. People gave me a party and wanted to give me gifts. I said that I didn't need gifts. Where would I put them in a little van? But what they could bring was a list of favorite friends from everywhere in the United States, so that any place in the country I could call and hear a friendly voice. I wasn't looking for housing or being fed or anything like that—just could we get together and say hi, and tell me about the community.

"Prior to that I had sold the house and gone off with just a sleeping bag I had borrowed and the car. I went to Colorado and visited my brother and sister-in-law and then went off to the Rockies and Utah and that area. There was something very restoring about being out in nature and sleeping in my tent on the ground, a very centering feeling of being connected to the earth. When I lived that way, there was an ambiance of being in a flow. I ate when I was hungry, went to bed at dark, and got up when I felt like it. I didn't need a watch. Time became liquid. It was rhythmic. It wasn't bounded by schedules and have-tos, you should do this, you have to do that. It became much more organic, in a way like the flow of the wind and the sun and the rain.

"I did a lot of hiking, not overnight, just day hiking, and got connected with the little animals that you see when you hike, and the flowers and the trees and the silence. Really, what I was doing was contending with loneliness and changing it into aloneness, because they are very different. The feeling was of embracing the solitude and being friend to my own inner being.

It was a sensation of being independent of anyone else, so that if I was ever in another relationship, it would not be from the impetus of clutching dependency but because of choice.

"I had been brought up by a very frightened mother with a very negative outlook. She looked under the bed and in the closets even if my dad was at home. With this background I had to overcome some of what I had ingested from her. So when I sold my house and everything and said good-bye, I was crawling out on the edge of a limb and cutting off the limb behind me. I didn't know what would happen, if I'd come up standing on my feet or flattened out or what. It was having to overcome the fears society puts on us of being out alone in a pup tent that can't be locked.

"But the choice was, Did I want to sit in my house with my cat in a secure place, or did I want to push my boundaries and learn to live vulnerably and take some risks in order to know myself better? In those days, 1978, women were not out alone on the road. It was a lifestyle I knew nothing about. I hated camping and was completely ignorant about it. When my family camped, I went to a motel. But I had a sure feeling that this was what I wanted to do. There was never any question in my mind that it was right for me.

"The only support I got from anyone was from my son, who said, 'You've got to do what you feel is going to make you happy.' Everyone else said things like, 'It's a dangerous world out there for women, and you are going alone?' And 'You mean you are selling your house, with nothing to come back to?'

"My choice was a choice for me; it wouldn't be for everyone else. People have to be attuned to themselves to know what direction their lives have to take. There were times I was scared, and then there were times I felt cooped up in a little car and tent. Sometimes I wanted to crawl up the walls of the tent. What the heck was I doing out there anyway, I thought, away from every living soul? Then all I needed to do was to look up at the stars, look at the mountains, or talk to a flower, and everything would be all right."

"How long have you been doing this?" I asked.

"I've been doing it fourteen years off and on," she answered. "Then I met the man I told you about and went back into practice. We moved to the town right next to the one I'd left. Here I'd been all over the United States and settled down right next door. We took some vacation time in Florida during that period, and I went to conferences, so I wasn't just settling down. Then when we separated four years later, I came back to the life of the road.

"The Keys again became my winter home. They never stopped calling me. The green of the trees and the bushes, the colors of the water and the mangroves; the islands are marching out, you know. They've got their fingers marching out on the waters. The Australian Pine trees are all around the beach areas. The trees are windswept. They are not indigenous to the Keys, but come from Australia. They all are kind of bending over with the westerly wind. But then I see this beauty where nobody else does. Like some people say how awful it is to drive through the desert, it's so barren and empty. I say, wow! there's so much to see in the desert.

"I often take my car and park under the trees. It is always nice and cool there. Sometimes there are ibises and herons and sandpipers, and there's all the seaweed that comes there. I go there sometimes before and after church or before a meeting, and it's somewhat the same feeling as going off on the land. It's a centering feeling, a feeling of oneness that is all around me, and any problems or frustrations melt away or evaporate."

Feeling that her sensuous oneness with nature seemed akin to what I have found in painters I have known, I asked Joan if she was an artist. "My life is my art," she answered. And indeed it is.

I found her an inspiration, this woman who has created a life of richness and harmony by following her own inner voice.

After talking with her, I started to go back to work on this book. Then I thought, "No, I'll write later. Now I want to walk by the ocean." So I did. I felt the soft sea breezes and watched the waves gently rippling on the shore. It felt good. And I was grateful to her. People like Joan are as good for others as they are for themselves.

Marie Coleman Nelson is a psychoanalyst of renown, who originated an ingenious technique of therapy called the Paradigmatic Approach. Marie is an unusual woman. She is a psychoanalyst who came up through the ranks without a college degree, a feat that was difficult then and all but impossible now. Apparently she and I share a similar philosophy concerning the subject matter of this chapter. According to her, she has always paid a great deal of attention to her inner voice, including the time it said, "Become a psychoanalyst!" And she did.[1]

As the story goes, one day after thirty-two years of private practice, the little voice cheerfully announced, "Time to move to Nairobi!"

"Move to Nairobi?" she exclaimed. "You can't be serious."

"I'm serious," said the voice flatly, and left.

So off she went to Africa, where she lived for many years. There she established a psychoanalytic clinic where none had existed before. She attended many African people who would have remained untreated had she not complied with her dream. She also trained new analysts to follow in her footsteps.

According to her, "This voice, which now says 'move along!' has always directed her toward further enlightenment and so brooks no denial." And because she listens to it, Marie is a modern-day heroine, who is to be emulated.

I live out my dreams in another manner, in addition to the professional change. Like Anaïs Nin, I get many of my ideas for writing from my dreams. When I wrote *Who Killed Virginia Woolf?* I had no idea of how to organize it, of what shape it should take. I considered it a psychological study of all aspects of her life, temporarily entitled *Virginia Woolf: Her Psychosis and Her Genius*. It in no way concentrated on her suicide. Shortly before the book was due at the publishers, I dreamed that I wrote a novel about why Woolf killed herself and who if anyone could have stopped her. For a brief period I considered actually writing that novel. Then I suddenly realized that I had already written it! I changed its organization to point up ideas about Woolf's suicide and then changed the name of the book. Then I turned it in for publication.

I have spoken in a previous chapter of how I was furious with my analyst and left her organization. This episode inspired another dream. In the midst of the leave-taking, I dreamed about Cinderella. I then wrote a spoof on analysis and my analyst called "A Modern Day Psychoanalytic Fable."[2] It was my way of expressing my anger with her, but not a single person picked that up. The article was beautifully received the first time it was published and was reprinted several times thereafter. When the piece was first published, newspapers used my contribution as the lead story on the journal. News about it was printed in over 250 papers all over the country, with headlines such as "Cinderella Was a Schizophrenic" and "Cinderella: Just a Case of Youthful Rebellion?" News items such as the following, from *USA Today* (January 6, 1984) were typical:

> Cinderella had a "schizophrenic mother and two sisters who were pathologically consumed with jealousy because of unsublimated sibling rivalry," concludes a psychological study. So it's no wonder that Cinderella left a glass slipper behind at the ball.

It was "clearly . . . an act of rebellion against the dictatorial regimentation of the domineering stepmother," writes Alma H. Bond, of the Institute for Psychoanalytic Training and Research. Her study is featured in the first issue of the *Journal of Polymorphous Perversity,* a magazine that seeks to inject "into the aging veins of psychology" a bit of humorous medicine. Sigmund Freud coined the phrase "polymorphous perversity" to describe the "many forms of deviation" in human behavior.

The funniest part of the whole thing is that despite the article's appearance in the *Journal of Polymorphous Perversity,* most of the newspaper stories didn't realize the article was meant as a spoof and reported it as "research."

A poem, "The Split," also was inspired by a dream.[3] The dream image was simply of my grandmother's old shoe, which my mother kept at the bottom of her bureau drawer. I never would have thought of writing the poem, one of the most meaningful I've ever composed, if it hadn't been inspired by my dream.

The philosophy of Faith Popcorn suggests that the path of pleasure apparently is coming of age. A headline in the Fort Lauderdale *Sun-Sentinel* (October 3, 1991) on Popcorn's book reads, "High-tech businesses will free minds, bodies," and states that in the nineties, "We'll finally learn how to maximize our technology—stretch our resources and save our souls." According to Ms. Popcorn a new upsurge in the search for gratification is taking place.[4] In contrast to earlier generations, who drew a distinct line between the pleasures permitted children and adults, some appropriate only for the first and others for the second, in the present decade adults are "redrawing the line." For example, unlike the "grown-ups of the past, adults of today can eat popsicles shamelessly and dress up for Halloween. She calls this concept "down-aging."

The kid inside us accompanies each adult on a shopping trip, where grown-up needs combine with the lack of impulse control of the child. She believes, "Our country is in search of a good time. Down-aging is the bridge by which we—adults of all ages—try to connect the carefree childhoods we remember (or at least the care-free baby-boom childhoods the media says we're *supposed* to remember) to the not-always-fun adulthood we find ourselves in now. . . . What we are doing is chasing after the promise and hope of childhood." She predicts that this generation will age "with a stylish vengeance, putting in more energy against growing old, and the way growing old makes us feel," than any that preceded us. She adds, "And spending more money than ever on doing it."

The author elaborates on this concept with many possible developments of the future. For example, she believes that in times to come, it may be unnecessary to leave the home to make our wishes come true. The day will arrive, according to her, when computers can take us on "mind-trips" to Africa, the Brazilian rain forest, or the Himalayas. Even more exciting than journeys through space may be those crossing the boundaries of time. Then mind-trips can take us back to the French Revolution, or return us to our childhood or that of our parents and grandparents.[5]

Imagine what such a trip would do for psychoanalysis! Instead of "reconstructions," in which the analyst deduces and gives "interpretations" to the patient about what his childhood was like, he will be able to go back and see what *really* happened. This would impart a conviction to the patient rarely achieved through words alone, which could either speed up the analytic process, or point out the inadequacies of the analyst.

An experience with my patient, Joseph, may serve as a "coming attraction" for this "invention." The young man had come to analysis to get rid of a painful phobia, fear of flying. In addition, at the age of three he had lost his father and had no conscious memory of him. Indeed, he felt he never had had a father at all.

A home movie had been shot when two-year-old Joseph and his parents were vacationing at the seashore. In the movie, Joseph and his father were sitting close together by the sea. The father's arm was around the child, and he was looking lovingly at him. Joseph watched the movie with tears in his eyes and said, "My father really loved me; I can tell by the way he is holding me and by the look in his eyes. I just remembered now—he always called me Yussele . . ." After watching this movie, he could discard the fiction that he never had a father.

Another result of the movie came about by surprise. In direct contrast to his phobic self, Joseph watched the small boy-that-was courageously leaping into giant waves of the sea. He realized that he was looking at himself as he was before the death of his father. Joseph understood beyond all doubt that by returning to his courageous self he would overcome his fear of flying. And so he did.

Such a mind-trip into the past, as fantasied by Popcorn, also might change the course of mourning, as permanent good-byes become a thing of the past. Instead, when we miss our dear departed, we can return to the time we spent together (as in the play *Our Town*). There we can have our loved ones back as often as we please.

Such an invention might contribute to the development of a different strain of mental illness. Individuals who prefer mind-trips to actual living, along with those who choose to remain fixed in childhood memories, may become as common as "couch potatoes" today.

Faith Popcorn also believes we are coming into The Age of the Brain, in which a strong epistemophilic instinct (an innate desire for knowledge) will come to the fore in our lives. She predicts that new "brain gyms" will form to exercise our thinking as we do our bodies today. She also speaks of "brain clubs" of the future, with mind games to sharpen our wits. If your dream is of becoming a "brain," then tomorrow is for you.

Is your hobby the main focus of your dreams? The future should help there, too. Author Popcorn envisions a "new career industry of noncareer advisers, planners, destinations," to help you develop the interests of your dreams. One can picture hordes of hobbyists enthusiastically pursuing their avocations. If life is a disappointment in one area, another avenue of gratification will await you in the wings.

Do you want to stay young-looking as long as you can, without the sudden disconcerting changes of plastic surgery? Popcorn imagines that "time-release, face-lift implants will de-age you ever so gradually." How else would you like your body to change? According to her, "Reconstructive surgery, to make you taller, bigger, stronger, straighter, with better sight and hearing" is another thing she thinks will come in the future.

Such a possibility would mean the rewriting of history as it *really* occurred, apart from the reports of partisan governments and newspapers. This would result in an extension of the manner in which television brings us to the site of history in the making, as in battles and presidential debates.

But best of all for the purposes of this book, Ms. Popcorn envisions a future that literally will make our dreams come true. She feels a new consulting business will arise devoted purely to implementing our dreams. There, individuals will uncover their secret wishes and then bring them to fruition. This will be done for selected time spans—for hours, for years, or a lifetime, depending on the wish of the customer. Whatever your dream career, whether in business, the arts, or the sciences, the organization will help you achieve it.

Freud contended that happiness consists of the fulfillment of childhood wishes. If Faith Popcorn's prophecies are borne out, then the world indeed will be a happier place, as more and more of us live out our childhood dreams.

One of the dreams we can follow today is that of living a longer, healthier life. The analyzed patient is frequently a good example of today's new "fitness freaks." For as the analyzed patient acquires a stronger ego, he finds the energy and wherewithal to look out for his own interests. Many ex-patients today are exercising, meditating, taking vitamins, and carefully moderating their diets. I myself do all of the above.

I have followed a well-researched health program for at least fifteen years. It is a rare day that I don't spend thirty minutes doing exercise of some sort—either swimming, running, biking, or riding an exercycle. I presently am considering learning the use of weights for an overinflated stomach. (I would like to try liposuction, but can't quite find the nerve.) I follow the Pritikin low-fat diet the best that I can, after spending a month at one of their centers to learn the particulars. In so doing, I lowered my cholesterol a hundred points and lost ten pounds in the bargain.

Is your goal to live forever? Well, you may not make it, but you certainly can try. It will result, at the very least, in improved health, better humor, a more youthful appearance, and the stamina to follow your star.

Why is it important to live out our inner dreams? Margaret Mahler spoke of the concept of "emotional refueling," when the exhausted infant or toddler turns to his or her mother for emotional sustenance. Sometimes just playing around her feet for a moment or two can send him back on his way. He knows what he needs to revive him. When his mother is unavailable, he often will just sit back and wait.

In life, whatever our ages, all of us get depleted at times, some more frequently than others. But most adults have no "mothers" around to help restore our good humor. Nor do we have analysts to serve this function after termination. Internalization of the analyst is certainly necessary and makes a successful termination possible. But as Freud intimated, it isn't always the complete solution for "common ordinary everyday unhappiness." Sometimes we need an additional form of emotional feeding.

Gratification in my work as analyst used to revive my flagging spirits, for I was madly in love with it. It was a rare working day that did not bring me at least a few moments of fulfillment. But when I gave up my practice, I had to renounce that method of refueling and was forced to find other means to fill the need.

What works for me now? I turn toward life. A good piece of writing might do it. And a book that is sold, a fine review, and/or a few loving words. These are wonderful, when the muse or the environment are kind enough to react as I would like. But the method is a bit risky, as it is too dependent on responses beyond our control.

But there is a way to get recharged, whatever is going on in the outside world. And that is to follow where impulse leads us. For every gratified wish ends with a charge of pleasure, whether we know it or not. (Just remember how it feels to eat when you are inordinately hungry.) Similarly, all satisfied wishes, great or small, bring their own quota of gratification.

Freud believed that this surge is of biological origin. He called it the Pleasure Principle, which dictates that gratification of instinctual wishes steers us away from death.[6] I agree. Do what makes you feel good, and it will keep you alive. Enough daily allotments of pleasure add up to a satisfied existence. In contrast, doing only what we think we should leaves us unfulfilled and fatigued, eventually leading to death. This simple method of reviving depleted spirits is the best means I know to help us live in gladness.

What are the obstacles that interfere with what we could do to enjoy life more fully? Uppermost are anxiety, guilt, shame, pain, and depression, along with the defenses people erect against them. Negative thinking and yielding to the pressures of the superego are particularly effective means of squelching pleasure.

So far as anxiety is concerned, there are many reasons to be frightened. There is the terror of failure that some of us are unable to endure. The dread of facing competition and losing. Or of winning, for those who are afraid of "castration" or its equivalent. Or the loss of love of people we need, who are jealous of our new success. And the fear of getting stuck in one's new interest, to the exclusion of family or loved ones. All of these anxieties can keep one emotionally frozen.

Freud said that the only way to cure a phobia is for the patient to face what he dreads. Such a person must find the courage to act despite his conscious anxiety. Then he may discover that something other than what he fears is lurking in his unconscious mind. This insight is often the turning point in mastering phobic anxiety. For how can we learn the danger is long past, if it ever existed at all, unless we take the risk? President Roosevelt put it well indeed when he informed the country, "There is nothing to fear but fear itself." He must have found this out the hard way.

I, too, found it out the hard way, after a car accident that left me impaired for months. When I first was able to go out of doors, I went with my nurse. Later, I walked alone with a cane. After a while I gave that up and moved ahead on shaking feet. But there was one challenge remaining that was harder to overcome. I was terrified to cross the street! I was petrified of being hit again by a car.

One day, I looked myself in the mirror and said, "This nonsense has got to stop. You're not going to stay a cripple for the rest of your life, if I have any say about it!" So I forced myself down to the corner to try to cross the street.

The light changed from green to red and back again, and still I could not move. I had the fantasy of stopping a passerby and pleading to be walked across the street. I thought maybe saying I was blind would do it. Fortunately I had the good grace to be embarrassed by this and tentatively put a toe into the street. Then I learned what my phobia was about.

When I first set foot off the curb, the scenery seemed to swirl about my head, as it surely did in the earliest stage of unconsciousness, when the taxi made contact with my body. I realize as I write this that I was experiencing another flashback.

When the swirling stopped, I looked across the street and didn't see any car. But I didn't believe my eyes. I knew I had looked already and no car was in sight. But I thought, "How can I be certain there isn't one that I missed? After all, I didn't see a car at the accident, and one was certainly there!"

I looked again. The traffic had passed. I still could see no car. "There *is* no car," I told myself and walked across the street.

It is ridiculous at my age to feel proud of crossing the street. But I do.

Negative thinking, whether your own or someone else's, is an aspect of depression that keeps many people unhappy.

Do you have a great idea for a story? The response will be, "It's been done before."

Do you want to go to the movies? Says the negative thinker, "We might as well not bother. It probably isn't any good."

Shall I try a new kind of casserole? A way to lose weight? A new way of keeping the books? "Don't waste your energy. My ———— (mother, father, brother) tried that, and it didn't work."

Jim Davis's "Garfield" (October 3, 1991), in the comic strip of that name, beautifully illustrates the pleasure-squashing nature of negative thinking. In the comic strip, Jon is singing as he drives Garfield and a rabbit chum in his car. Garfield says, "Jon's really enjoying this drive . . . entirely too much." Then turning to his buddy, he says, "One of us has to get carsick."

The dictates of the superego frequently prevent people from following their impulses. A good example is given in the case of John Jones (chapter 5), in which a rigid conscience kept John virtually paralyzed. We can see it all around us, in the fashion of "real men don't eat quiche." Many of us get attacks of the "shoulds" when it comes to pleasing ourselves. We "shouldn't" spend the money," We "should" have the Smiths in for dinner (even though you hate the Smiths). We should make that telephone call (when your body is crying for sleep). We "should" stay home sending bills (that new movie will wait.) We "should" buy a new refrigerator (instead of going to Europe.) Another form the "shoulds" sickness takes is, "People will think we are crazy, selfish, effeminate, not nice, and so forth, if we do what we really want to."

My husband was very good at managing this sort of thing, which I found very helpful. We had a seashore house on Long Beach Island, New Jersey, when our children were growing up. Many people would drop in for a stay at the shore. I usually was happy to see them, but soon found I was spending much of my time in the kitchen. Rudy put up a notice on the refrigerator door, saying:

"You are welcome to stay here, but it is Alma's vacation, too. Feel free to cook if you like, but please take responsibility for your own meals." To the best of my knowledge, no one was ever insulted.

Another reason for pleasure squelching is that it leads to embarrassment. People are ashamed of looking silly, or of feeling like a baby. Or of having ignoble thoughts. Many are mortified to harbor even harmless fantasies. Shame plays a particularly inhibiting role in sex. Some people are abashed to admit that the thought of such and such a sexual act is exciting to them. Others keep harmless pleasures in the realm of fantasy, when it could be acted on. This is not as common as it was before the sixties, but still exists in the minds of many. Shame can be a necessary and healthy feeling when it prevents dangerous and hurtful actions. But much of what we were taught as being wrong is now outmoded thinking, for example, harmless sexual activity between consenting adults. By-passing outdated embarrassment and following instinctual impulses could lead to increased satisfaction in many lives today.

One of my earliest woman patients overcame her embarrassment enough to inform her husband that a particular touch would give her sexual pleasure. He requested that she ask me if it was all right for a woman to tell a man what she wants in the sexual act. When I write this now, it seems unbelievable that this kind of thinking was operant only a few generations ago, when women were not "supposed" to be sexually active.

Styles in principles change, along with sexual mores. Many "rules" of conduct are foolish and unnecessary, but most people who are brought up with them take them to be fact. Look, for example, at how the stigma attached to losing virginity or being a "pinko" has virtually disappeared from our society. Who wears white gloves to the market anymore or goes swimming in full dress? What was required for respectability just a few decades back is now considered peculiar. Some fortunate people were always relatively free to choose what ethical paths to follow. We would all do well to emulate them. Those who follow their instincts whenever they can are less constrained by fads of conscience. They are freer from the unnecessary restrictions of the times and able to lead richer, fuller, more gratifying lives. Perhaps the solution to outgrowing Freud's "ordinary everyday unhappiness" is just as simple as that.

Notes

Chapter 1

1. *Miami Herald*, 31 March 1992.
2. Karen Horney, *Self Analysis* (New York: W. W. Norton and Co., 1942).
3. A. Bond, D. Franco, and A. K. Richards, *Dream Portrait* (Madison, Conn.: International Universities Press, 1992).
4. William Wordsworth, "The World Is too Much with Us; Late and Soon."
5. *Miami Herald*, 20 September 1991.
6. Sigmund Freud, *Civilization and Its Discontents*, 21 (London: Hogarth Press and the Institute of Psychoanalysis, 1930), 76.

Chapter 2

1. Marie Coleman Nelson, "Comments," *Voices*, 13, no. 4 (1977), 16–17.
2. Bond, Franco, Richards, *Dream Portrait*, 3.
3. Maxwell Gittleson, "Analytic Aphorisms," *Psychoanalytic Quarterly*, 36 (1967), 262.
4. Jack Novick, "The Timing of Termination," *International Review of Psychoanalysis*, 15 (1988), 305–18.
5. Ernst A. Ticho, "Termination of Psychoanalysis: Treatment Goals, Life Goals," *Psychoanalytic Quarterly*, 41 (1972), 315.
6. Gittleson, "Analytic Aphorisms," 260.
7. Hartlaub, Martin, and Rhine, "Recontact with the Analyst Following Termination: A Survey of 71 Cases," *Journal of the American Psychoanalytic Assn.*, 34 (1986), 895–910.
8. Arnold Z. Pfeffer, "The Meaning of the Analyst after Analysis: A Contribution to the Theory of Therapeutic Results," *Journal of the American Psychoanalytic Assn.*, 11 (1963), 229–94.
9. Sigmund Freud, *The Standard Edition of the Complete Psychological Works of Sigmund Freud*, 23 (London: Hogarth Press, 1964), 224–25.

10. Arnold Z. Pfeffer, "A Procedure for Evaluating the Results of Psycho-analysis: A Preliminary Report," *Journal of the Psychoanalytic Assn.*, 7, no. 3 (July 1959), 30–32.

11. Arnold Z. Pfeffer, "Memories of Positive Experiences in the Resolution of Conflicts: Illustrated in a Case of Hysteria," *Journal of the American Psychoanalytic Assn.*, 28 (1980), 309–30.

12. S. Firestein, "Termination of Psychoanalysis of Adults: A Review of the Literature," *Journal of the American Psychoanalytic Assn.*, 20 (1974), 873–95.

13. Bond, Franco, and Richards, *Dream Portrait*, 57–131.

14. Ticho, "Termination of Psychoanalysis," 315–32.

15. J. Cavenar and J. Nash, "The Dream as a Signal for Termination," *Journal of the American Psychoanalytic Assn.*, 24 (1976), 425–36.

16. R. Gillman, "The Termination Phase in Clinical Practice: A Survey of 48 Completed Cases, *Psychoanalytic Inquiry*, 2 (1982), 463–72.

17. Martin S. Bergmann, "The Intrapsychic and Communicative Aspects of the Dream," *International Journal of Psychoanalysis*, 47 (1966), 356–63.

18. H. Gaskill, "The Closing Phase of the Psychoanalytic Treatment of Adults and the Goals of Psychoanalysis: The Myth of Perfectibility," *International Journal of Psychoanalysis*, 61 (1980), 11–21.

19. Leon Grinberg, "The Closing Phase of the Psychoanalytical Treatment of Adults and the Goals of Psychoanalysis," *International Journal of Psychoanalysis*, 61 (1980), 25–38.

20. Ticho, "Termination of Psychoanalysis: Treatment Goals, Life Goals," 315–33.

21. Jerome Oremland, "A Specific Dream During the Termination Phase of a Successful Psychoanalysis," *Journal of the American Psychoanalytic Assn.*, 21 (1973), 285–302.

22. G. Blanck and R. Blanck, "The Contribution of Ego Psychology to Understanding the Process of Termination in Psychoanalysis and Psychotherapy," *Journal of the American Psychoanalytic Assn.*, 4, no. 36 (1989), 961–84.

Chapter 5

1. This case is discussed much more thoroughly in *Dream Portrait*.

2. W. Meissner, *Internalization in Psychoanalysis* (New York: International Universities Press, 1981).

3. Jacob Arlow, keynote speaker, *The Primal Scene Symposium*, Biscayne Bay, Fla., 1982.

Chapter 6

1. Sorry, Sally, but I am unable to carry out your request. I just couldn't publicly divulge the many confidences that you trusted me with during your analysis.

Chapter 7

1. I am grateful to Guy Blaine, of the United Universalist Church, for bringing out the difference between group therapy and mutual support groups in his booklet *Mutual Support Groups*.

2. Alma H. Bond, "Sadomasochistic Patterns in an Eighteen-Month-Old Child," *International Journal of Psychoanalysis*, 48, part 4 (1967), 597–602.

Chapter 8

1. Not her real name.

2. One of the members of the group told me that this is incorrect, that Ruth Dreamdigger is the person members turn to when they need help with a dream.

3. In using the Gestalt system, the dreamer applies each part of the dream to himself or herself. For example, if you dream about an art museum, you say, "I am an art museum. I am filled with visions of beauty, etc." This method helps the dreamer get in touch with unexplored parts of the personality.

Chapter 9

1. Ann Faraday, *Dream Power* (Calif.: Berkeley Publishing Corp., 1972), 17.

2. Michael E. Murray and Martha L. Murray, "Senoi Dream Therapy," in *Voices*, 14, no. 1 (1978), 36–48.

3. Fr. Charles Thomas Cayce, "Mind Power Opportunities," *Bottom Line*, 15 October 1991, 3.

4. Ella Freeman Sharpe, *Dream Analysis* (London: Hogarth Press, 1951), 192–99.

Chapter 10

1. Marie Coleman Nelson, "Tired? No—Just Metamorphosis," *Voices*, 15, no. 2 (1979), 44–45.

2. Alma H. Bond, "A Modern Day Psychoanalytic Fable," *The Worm Runners Digest*, 12, no. 2 (1970–71), 101–103..

3. Alma H. Bond, "The Split," *Voices* (Summer, 1975), 59.

4. Faith Popcorn, *The Popcorn Report* (New York: Doubleday Currency, 1991), 60–61.

5. Popcorn, *The Popcorn Report*, 187–88.

6. Sigmund Freud, *The Standard Edition of the Complete Psychological Works of Sigmund Freud*, 18, "Beyond the Pleasure Principle," (London: Hogarth Press, 1955).